SCIENTIFIC AMERICAN EXPLORES BIG IDEAS

Navigating Anxiety & Depression

The Editors of *Scientific American*

SCIENTIFIC AMERICAN EDUCATIONAL PUBLISHING

New York

Published in 2023 by Scientific American Educational Publishing
in association with **The Rosen Publishing Group**
29 East 21st Street, New York, NY 10010

Contains material from Scientific American®, a division of Springer Nature America, Inc., reprinted by permission, as well as original material from The Rosen Publishing Group®.

First Edition

Scientific American
Lisa Pallatroni: Project Editor

Rosen Publishing
Erica Grove: Compiling Editor
Michael Moy: Senior Graphic Designer

Cataloging-in-Publication Data
Names: Scientific American.
Title: Navigating anxiety and depression / Scientific American.
Description: New York : Scientific American Educational, 2023. | Series: Scientific american explores big ideas| Includes bibliographic information, glossary and index.
Identifiers: ISBN 9781684169337 (pbk) | ISBN 9781684169344 (library bound) | ISBN 9781684169351 (ebook)
Subjects: LCSH: Anxiety– Juvenile literature | Depression, Mental– Juvenile literature | Mental health– Juvenile literature
Classification: LCC BF724.3.A57 S35 2023 | DDC 616.85 -dc23

Manufactured in the United States of America
Websites listed were live at the time of publication.

Cover: Stanislaw Mikulski/Shutterstock.com

CPSIA Compliance Information: Batch # SACS23.
For Further Information contact Rosen Publishing at 1-800-237-9932.

CONTENTS

INTRODUCTION

Anxiety and depression have affected people throughout human history, but despite how common these conditions are there is still much about them that is misunderstood. In fact, some would argue that depression and anxiety–among other mental health conditions–are becoming increasingly common, creating a mental health crisis. A number of variables are blamed for this uptick, including escalating climate change, racism, the COVID-19 pandemic, and increased social media use. However, while the causes of anxiety and depression may seem to be multiplying, the potential treatment options for these conditions also continue to expand. These treatments cover the spectrum of mental health care, ranging from new types and ways of delivering behavioral therapy to new drugs and medical treatments.

The articles in this book attempt to catalogue and examine the knowledge and attitudes surrounding these mental health conditions today. They present contemporary opinions and studies on the causes of anxiety and depression, and consider a range of potential new treatments for these conditions. Section 1, "The Evolving Landscape of Anxiety and Depression," examines how our understanding of these conditions has shifted in recent years. Section 2, "Causes of Anxiety and Depression in Today's World," looks at how conditions of present-day society affect mental health. Section 3, "Novel Medical and Drug Treatments for Anxiety and Depression," examines new medical procedures and medications–as well as drugs that already existed but were not used to treat these conditions–that are presented as potential new treatment options. Section 4, "New Therapies and Lifestyle Changes for Anxiety and Depression," looks at new types of behavioral therapy, new ways of offering therapy, and changes that could be made in daily life to help fight anxiety and depression. Some of the therapies examined in these articles may even present the opportunity for a brighter tomorrow in the field of mental health.

Section 1: The Evolving Landscape of Anxiety and Depression

Expanding Mental Health Care Is a Medical Necessity

By the Editors of *Scientific American*

It is a classic refrain in psychological research: people are more resilient than they realize. The acute upheaval of the early pandemic era led to a spike in depression and anxiety. A year or so later those numbers appeared, in many studies, to return to prepandemic levels, reflecting the science that says most of us tend to bounce back from traumatic events. But the longer-term disruptions, losses and volatile shifts from hope to fear to languishing are harder to parse. COVID has already killed or disabled millions, deepened economic insecurity and racial inequality, and forced radical adaptations to daily life; its serious effects on mental health and well-being very likely will continue and in ways still unknown.

In 2020, the U.S. Congress responded to the mental health crisis by providing temporary funding for services and forcing the expansion of insurance coverage. These emergency measures must be permanently extended to meet emerging needs–and expanded to tackle long-standing and systemic inadequacies in care. In September the American Psychological Association called on Congress to do just that, along with mandating increases in the number of mental health providers. The *Lancet* COVID-19 Commission Task Force on Mental Health, meanwhile, wrote that the pandemic "offers a critical opportunity to invest in and strengthen mental health care systems to achieve a 'parity of esteem,' meaning that someone who is mentally ill should have equal access to evidence-based treatment as someone who is physically ill."

The idea that mental health is less legitimate than physical health has led to paltry insurance coverage, a scarcity of counseling professionals, and regulatory hurdles that make finding care especially difficult in rural and other underserved locations. Yet research has continued to reveal that the separation between mind and body is a false one: chronic emotional distress can significantly increase the chances of developing serious physical disease.

Talk therapy is especially well-suited to telemedicine, which has grown rapidly as an emergency measure and can be adopted as a true alternative to clinical settings. Video-based sessions work as well as, if not better than, in-person sessions, perhaps because it is easier for people to show up consistently. Insurance companies must continue to cover virtual appointments. Equally important are systemic policy changes to bolster socioeconomic support: it is harder to cope with emotional distress when also worrying about financial security.

Young people, in particular, have been hurt by pandemic disruptions. Many are struggling to see a hopeful future for themselves—a key to resilience. Researchers agree that preempting behavioral problems and mental illness makes more sense than beginning treatment after a crisis. One way to proactively reach more young people is to teach cognitive-behavioral therapy and mindfulness in schools. Using standard textbooks and trainings, students could learn to self-soothe, regulate emotions and form healthy coping mechanisms for stress. Such institutional programs would be especially helpful for the more than two million children worldwide who have lost a caregiver to COVID.

Two other groups of people need dedicated focus: those who were infected with COVID and those who treat them. In a recent global review, more than half of people who tested positive report symptoms of so-called long COVID, including brain fog, lethargy and depression. Approximately one in three survivors has been diagnosed with a generalized anxiety disorder and one in eight with post-traumatic stress disorder. Clinicians must prepare for a surge of patients who need psychiatric treatment. Nurses, doctors and other health-care workers, too, need more institutional support; many still avoid speaking up about psychological distress, fearing (often rightly) that it could jeopardize their jobs. Ending the stigma of seeking care would help acknowledge the traumas of COVID, as well as the burnout that was already endemic in the profession.

The "end" of the pandemic must not signal a return to the status quo, if only because it is not the only global force threatening emotional resilience. Severe wildfire seasons, rapidly intensifying hurricanes and deluges of rain—all consequences of climate change—mean that more and more people are experiencing terrifying disasters and loss. Such upheavals will keep overlapping rather than dissipating. It is long past time to prioritize mental health as essential to overall health. Fostering resilience in a world of accelerating uncertainty depends on it.

Susceptibility to Mental Illness May Have Helped Humans Adapt over the Millennia

By Dana G. Smith

Nearly one in five Americans currently suffers from a mental illness, and roughly half of us will be diagnosed with one at some point in our lives. Yet, these occurrences may have nothing to do with a genetic flaw or a traumatic event.

Randolph Nesse, a professor of life sciences at Arizona State University, attributes high rates of psychiatric disorders to natural selection operating on our genes without paying heed to our emotional well-being. What's more, the selective processes took place thousands of years before the unique stresses of modern urban existence, leading to a mismatch between our current environment and the one for which we were adapted.

In his new book, *Good Reasons for Bad Feelings: Insights from the Frontier of Evolutionary Psychiatry*, Nesse recruits the framework of evolutionary medicine to make a case for why psychiatric disorders persist despite their debilitating consequences. Some conditions, like depression and anxiety, may have developed from normal, advantageous emotions. Others, such as schizophrenia or bipolar disorder, result from genetic mutations that may have been beneficial in less extreme manifestations of a trait. *Scientific American* spoke to Nesse about viewing psychiatry through an evolutionary lens to help both patients and clinicians.

[An edited transcript of the interview follows.]

Q: A big part of your thesis is that some traits of mental disorders can be advantageous or adaptive—a depressed mood, for instance, might be beneficial for us. Where do you draw the line between the normal spectrum of emotion and pathology?

A: You can't decide what's normal and what's abnormal until you understand the ordinary function of any trait—whether it's vomiting or cough or fever or nausea. You start with its normal function and in what situation it gives selected advantages. But there are a lot of places where natural selection has shaped mechanisms that express these defenses when they're not needed, and very often that emotional response is painful and unnecessary in that instance. Then there's a category of emotions that make us feel bad but benefit our genes. A lot of sexual longings [extramarital affairs or unrequited love], for instance, don't do us any good at all, but they might potentially benefit our genes in the long run.

So it's not saying that these emotions are useful all the time. It's the capacity for these emotions that is useful. And the regulation systems [that control emotion] were shaped by natural selection—so sometimes they're useful for us, sometimes they're useful for our genes, sometimes it's false alarms in the system and sometimes the brain is just broken. We shouldn't try to make any global generalizations, we should examine every patient individually and try to understand what's going on.

Q: In the book you suggest that low mood could be advantageous for two very separate reasons. One of the motivators is to shift strategies to escape a situation, and the other is to have people stop striving and conserve energy. How do you reconcile these opposing theories?

A: It's intuitively obvious that when an organism, not just a human, is wasting energy trying to pursue a goal and not making progress, it's best to wait and slow down and not waste energy. Then if nothing works—even when you try to find a new strategy—to give up that goal completely.

Of course for we humans, it's not always seeking out nuts and fruits and berries. We're trying to garner social resources, and that creates inordinate complexity and competition. And it's not so easy to give up looking for a marital partner or give up looking for a job; we can't just do that. These moods are guiding us to try to put effort into things that are going to work instead of things that are not going to work. That doesn't mean we should just follow them, but it does mean respecting them more and trying to figure out what they might be telling us about the things we're trying to do in life.

Q: Could treating someone with antidepressants be disadvantageous, then, if low mood is a normal coping mechanism?

A: Evolutionary psychology I see very much as a subset of evolutionary medicine in general. And one of the most practically useful insights of evolutionary medicine is that we should be analyzing the costs and benefits of blocking every single defensive response, whether it's fever or pain or nausea or vomiting or cough or fatigue. Usually because of the "smoke detector" principle you can block these things safely. [The principle is Nesse's theory that an overactive fight-or-flight response that causes false alarms–and potentially an anxiety disorder–is better than an underactive system that fails to alert you to danger and could result in death.]

Some people have said that because I say low mood can be useful, I think we shouldn't treat it with medications. I say exactly the opposite. Once you know that low mood is usually not helpful even though it's normal, you go ahead and relieve it however you can.

Q: You talk a lot about genes in the book, but also how we've come up short in looking for genes for depression or schizophrenia. What role do you think genes play in the evolutionary model of the mental illness?

A: First of all, there are two very different categories of illness that should be kept separate. One is the emotional disorders, which are potentially normal, useful responses to situations. And in all such responses, variability and sensitivity are influenced by lots of different genes.

There are also mental disorders that are the most severe ones that are just plain old genetic diseases: bipolar disease and autism and schizophrenia. They're genetic diseases, and whether you get them or not is overwhelmingly dependent on what genes you have. But why would a strong, inheritable trait that cuts fitness by half not be selected against? I think this is one of the deepest mysteries in psychiatry.

Q: What could be some of the potential benefit of these latter conditions or other uses for these genes?

A: For bipolar disease, the reduction in the number of offspring is not very great at all, so it might be that there's not much selection acting there. And what if a tendency to be bipolar resulted in having even more children? What would happen then? Well it [the gene] would become universal, even though it caused bipolar disease. Maybe something like this has already happened. Maybe many of us have tendencies to grand ambitions and mood swings that probably aren't good for us but might lend to grand successes on occasion, and that might lead to great reproductive success.

Then there's the "cliff edge" effect, which is the possibility that some traits are pushed very far towards a peak that's close to a place where fitness collapses for a few percent of the population. This could be a new way of looking at all of these diseases in which we have many genes with small effects. It might be that what we should be looking for is the fitness landscape and not assume that the genes involved are abnormal.

Q: What do you hope patients or clinicians can gain from reading your book?

A: I find many of my patients feel like they're abnormal if they are told, "You have an anxiety disorder, you have a depressive disorder." Talk with them a little bit about the fact that there are advantages to anxiety and that low moods might have meaning. It might not just be something that's broken in you, it might be that your emotions are trying to tell you something. I think that makes many people feel less like they're defective.

About the Author

Dana Smith is a freelance science writer specializing in brains and bodies. She has written for Scientific American, *the* Atlantic, *the* Guardian, *NPR,* Discover, *and* Fast Company, *among other outlets. In a previous life, she earned a Ph.D. in experimental psychology from the University of Cambridge.*

Brain Imaging Identifies Different Types of Depression

By Esther Landhuis

For much of her life Anne Dalton battled depression. She seldom spoke with people. She stayed home a lot. The days dragged on with a sense of "why bother?" for the 61-year-old from New Jersey who used to work at a Wall Street investment firm. After trying more than a dozen combinations of antidepressant drugs to no avail, things got so bad two years ago that Dalton went in for electroconvulsive therapy—in which "basically they shock your brain," as she puts it.

Like Dalton, most of the estimated 16 million U.S. adults who have reported a major depressive episode in the past year find little relief even after several months on antidepressants—a problem that some researchers say may stem from the way mental illness is diagnosed.

Objective lab tests can physically confirm heart disease or cancer, but psychiatric conditions are classified somewhat vaguely as clusters of reported symptoms. Doctors consider people clinically depressed if they say they have low mood and meet at least four additional criteria from an overall list of nine. Yet depression can manifest differently from person to person: One might be putting on pounds and sleeping much of the time whereas another might be losing weight, feeling anxious and finding it difficult to sit still, says Conor Liston, a neuroscientist and psychiatrist at Weill Cornell Medicine. "The fact that we lump people together like this has been a big obstacle in understanding the neurobiology of depression," Liston explains.

New research published by Liston and colleagues in *Nature Medicine* seems to point toward a long-sought goal in psychiatry—biological markers to distinguish different kinds of depression. The researchers used a noninvasive technique called functional magnetic resonance imaging (fMRI) to measure the strength of connections between neural circuits in the brain. Analyzing fMRI scans from more than 1,000 people, of whom about 40 percent had been diagnosed as depressive, the team identified four subtypes of depression. If confirmed in additional studies, the findings could enable clearer diagnoses and pave the way for personalized therapies targeting brain networks found to be awry in individual patients.

The *Nature Medicine* study, published in December, grew out of a curious observation Liston made during his earlier work on stress. As an MD/PhD student he conducted experiments in rats and found that stress reduced neural connections in a brain area called the prefrontal cortex, which controls mental flexibility–the ability to adapt one's thinking to new situations, and to overcome habitual responses.

Liston also studied stress in students preparing for their medical licensing exams. Like the rats, stressed students displayed abnormal electrical activity in brain circuits that involve mental flexibility. (Luckily, getting a month off after the high-stakes test allowed their faulty networks to recover, suggesting the brain is more resilient than expected.) In a later study that Liston conducted with Weill Cornell psychiatrist Marc Dubin, the brain-imaging researchers detected similar network changes in people who are depressed–but only in a small subset of these patients.

That intrigued Liston. It seemed to him that stress, or something like it, throws off the flexibility circuits in certain depressed individuals–whereas other people become depressed for different reasons. That would be consistent with the view that depression "is not just one biological thing," Liston says.

That idea aligns with a new set of priorities called Research Domain Criteria, launched in 2008 by the National Institute of Mental Health to encourage scientists studying mental illness to drill down to core mechanisms rather than placing disorders under blanket labels. This shift in thinking has invigorated the search for a range of biomarkers for depression–toxic free radicals, the stress hormone cortisol and even epigenetics (environmental triggers that switch genes on and off). "Depression is too complex to be reduced to a single biomarker," says Nunzio Pomara, a professor of psychiatry and pathology at New York University School of Medicine who was not involved in Liston's work. At this point no individual biomarker is considered good enough to use routinely as a clinical tool, but researchers hope the best ones could someday be combined to improve diagnosis and treatment of depression and other psychiatric conditions.

To look for new biomarkers, the Weill Cornell team used a method called resting-state fMRI to check for differences in brain connectivity between depressed and healthy people. The procedure scans the brain while a person lies on a bed for five minutes–but the resulting data is complex and messy. Brain fMRI measurements are sensitive to minuscule differences between subjects such as whether people look around the room or shut their eyes during the scan. To do a rigorous analysis, Liston knew he needed a mountain of data, far more than he could collect on his own. "I went around and begged a lot of people I knew, and some I didn't know, who had collected data the same way we did," he says. He ended up with brain scans from 1,188 individuals–some healthy, some depressed–studied at 17 research sites worldwide. Having that much data yielded enough statistical power that "we didn't have to constrain ourselves to [analyzing] just a few regions" of the brain, Liston says. For each subject the team examined 258 brain areas, measuring how strongly each connects with other areas.

Using an approach called machine learning, in which a computer teaches itself to find patterns in the data, the analysis showed depressed people could be distinguished from healthy controls based on brain connectivity differences measured by fMRI in the limbic and frontostriatal areas. The limbic system controls emotions and frontostriatal networks help coordinate motor and cognitive functions. One brain area, called the subgenual cingulate cortex, has unusually strong connections with other regions of the brain in people who are depressed.

Prior imaging studies had implicated these areas in depression, and some of those analyses suggested connectivity measures could differentiate between depressed and healthy people. But the Weill Cornell team is believed to be the first to confirm findings in a separate population–an additional analysis that is seen as a mark of scientific rigor. "This represents an exciting approach," Pomara says. "It sets the stage for future studies." He notes, though, that brain connectivity data does not address the underlying biology of depression. It does not explain what is going on at the level of cells and chemical messengers–the sorts of discoveries that guide development of new drugs. Still, he says the new fMRI analysis "goes beyond what has been done with similar neuroimaging techniques" by identifying four kinds of depressed patients on the basis of connectivity problems. Most imaging analyses merely distinguished healthy and depressed people.

In the new study, the fMRI-based subdivisions could be linked to particular symptoms. Patients falling into the first two subtypes reported more fatigue whereas those in the other two reported more trouble feeling pleasure. This subtyping has implications not just for diagnosis but potentially for nonpharmaceutical treatment. Relative to groups two and four, people with depression subtype 1 were three times as likely to benefit from a newer therapy known as transcranial magnetic stimulation, or TMS. This technology uses a magnet to produce small electric currents in brain areas affected by depression. Although the procedure is gaining popularity, it is generally reserved for patients who have not responded to conventional antidepressants–people like Dalton.

In 2015, when Dalton became suicidal but felt she could not stand the memory loss associated with electroconvulsive therapy, she came to Dubin's office for TMS. Her sister drove her in for the half-hour procedure five days a week for four weeks. By the middle of the second week, "something lifted from my brain," Dalton says. "I laughed easier. I didn't have those suicidal thoughts. Everything wasn't lost to me. I thought, okay, I can do this. I can get up every day and get going."

Dubin says TMS could one day be tuned to treat patients with different depression subtypes. After scanning a patient's brain with fMRI, as done in the recent study, a physician could adjust the TMS magnet so it aims directly at the brain areas with abnormal connectivity in that person. "In the next five years we could be doing that," he says.

About the Author

Esther Landhuis is a freelance science and health journalist based in the San Francisco Bay Area. Follow her on Twitter @elandhuis

Bad News for the Highly Intelligent

By David Z. Hambrick, Madeline Marquardt

There are advantages to being smart. People who do well on standardized tests of intelligence–IQ tests–tend to be more successful in the classroom and the workplace. Although the reasons are not fully understood, they also tend to live longer, healthier lives, and are less likely to experience negative life events such as bankruptcy.

Now there's some bad news for people in the right tail of the IQ bell curve. In a study just published in the journal *Intelligence*, Pitzer College researcher Ruth Karpinski and her colleagues emailed a survey with questions about psychological and physiological disorders to members of Mensa. A "high IQ society," Mensa requires that its members have an IQ in the top 2 percent. For most intelligence tests, this corresponds to an IQ of about 132 or higher. (The average IQ of the general population is 100.) The survey of Mensa's highly intelligent members found that they were more likely to suffer from a range of serious disorders.

The survey covered mood disorders (depression, dysthymia and bipolar), anxiety disorders (generalized, social and obsessive-compulsive), attention-deficit hyperactivity disorder and autism. It also covered environmental allergies, asthma and autoimmune disorders. Respondents were asked to report whether they had ever been formally diagnosed with each disorder or suspected they suffered from it. With a return rate of nearly 75 percent, Karpinski and her colleagues compared the percentage of the 3,715 respondents who reported each disorder to the national average.

The biggest differences between the Mensa group and the general population were seen for mood disorders and anxiety disorders. More than a quarter (26.7 percent) of the sample reported that they had been formally diagnosed with a mood disorder, while 20 percent reported an anxiety disorder–far higher than the national averages of around 10 percent for each. The differences were smaller, but still statistically significant and practically meaningful, for most of the other disorders. The prevalence of environmental allergies was triple the national average (33 percent vs. 11 percent).

To explain their findings, Karpinski and her colleagues propose the *hyper brain/hyper body theory*. This theory holds that, for all of its advantages, being highly intelligent is associated with psychological and physiological "overexcitabilities," or OEs. A concept introduced by the Polish psychiatrist and psychologist Kazimierz Dabrowski in the 1960s, an OE is an unusually intense reaction to an environmental threat or insult. This can include anything from a startling sound to confrontation with another person.

Psychological OEs include a heightened tendency to ruminate and worry, whereas physiological OEs arise from the body's response to stress. According to the hyper brain/hyper body theory, these two types of OEs are more common in highly intelligent people and interact with each other in a "vicious cycle" to cause both psychological and physiological dysfunction. For example, a highly intelligent person may overanalyze a disapproving comment made by a boss, imagining negative outcomes that simply wouldn't occur to someone less intelligent. That may trigger the body's stress response, which may make the person even more anxious.

The results of this study must be interpreted cautiously because they are correlational. Showing that a disorder is more common in a sample of people with high IQs than in the general population doesn't prove that high intelligence is the cause of the disorder. It's also possible that people who join Mensa differ from other people in ways other than just IQ. For example, people preoccupied with intellectual pursuits may spend less time than the average person on physical exercise and social interaction, both of which have been shown to have broad benefits for psychological and physical health.

All the same, Karpinski and her colleagues' findings set the stage for research that promises to shed new light on the link between intelligence and health. One possibility is that associations between intelligence and health outcomes reflect *pleiotropy*, which occurs when a gene influences seemingly unrelated traits. There is already some evidence to suggest that this is the case. In a 2015 study, Rosalind Arden and her colleagues concluded that the association between IQ and longevity is mostly explained by genetic factors.

From a practical standpoint, this research may ultimately lead to insights about how to improve people's psychological and physical well-being. If overexcitabilities turn out to be the mechanism underlying the IQ-health relationship, then interventions aimed at curbing these sometimes maladaptive responses may help people lead happier, healthier lives.

About the Authors

David Z. Hambrick is a professor in the department of psychology at Michigan State University. His research focuses on individual differences in cognition and the development of expertise.

Madeline Marquardt is an undergraduate student at MSU majoring in neuroscience and professional writing.

Is Depression Just Bad Chemistry?

By Hal Arkowitz, Scott O. Lilienfeld

A commercial sponsored by Pfizer, the drug company that manufactures the antidepressant Zoloft, asserts, "While the cause [of depression] is unknown, depression may be related to an imbalance of natural chemicals between nerve cells in the brain. Prescription Zoloft works to correct this imbalance." Using advertisements such as this one, pharmaceutical companies have widely promoted the idea that depression results from a chemical imbalance in the brain.

The general idea is that a deficiency of certain neurotransmitters (chemical messengers) at synapses, or tiny gaps, between neurons interferes with the transmission of nerve impulses, causing or contributing to depression. One of these neurotransmitters, serotonin, has attracted the most attention, but many others, including norepinephrine and dopamine, have also been granted supporting roles in the story.

Much of the general public seems to have accepted the chemical imbalance hypothesis uncritically. For example, in a 2007 survey of 262 undergraduates, psychologist Christopher M. France of Cleveland State University and his colleagues found that 84.7 percent of participants found it "likely" that chemical imbalances cause depression. In reality, however, depression cannot be boiled down to an excess or deficit of any particular chemical or even a suite of chemicals. "Chemical imbalance is sort of last-century thinking. It's much more complicated than that," neuroscientist Joseph Coyle of Harvard Medical School was quoted as saying in a blog by National Public Radio's Alix Spiegel.

Indeed, it is very likely that depression stems from influences other than neurotransmitter abnormalities. Among the problems correlated with the disease are irregularities in brain structure and function, disturbances in neural circuitry, and various psychological contributions, such as life stressors. Of course, all these influences ultimately operate at the level of physiology, but understanding them requires explanations from other vantage points.

Are Your Chemicals out of Balance?

Perhaps the most frequently cited evidence in support of the chemical imbalance hypothesis is the effectiveness of antidepressants, many of which increase the amounts of serotonin and other neurotransmitters at synapses. Zoloft, Prozac and similar selective serotonin reuptake inhibitors (SSRIs) result in such an increase and can often relieve depression, at least when it is severe. As a result, many believe that a deficiency in serotonin and other neurotransmitters causes the disorder. But just because a drug reduces symptoms of a disease does not mean that those symptoms were caused by a chemical problem the drug corrects. Aspirin alleviates headaches, but headaches are not caused by a deficiency of aspirin.

Evidence against the hypothesis comes from the efficacy of a newly developed antidepressant, Stablon (Tianeptine), which *decreases* levels of serotonin at synapses. Indeed, in different experiments, activation or blockage of certain serotonin receptors has improved or worsened depression symptoms in an unpredictable manner. A further challenge to the chemical imbalance hypothesis is that many depressed people are not helped by SSRIs. In a 2009 review article psychiatrist Michael Gitlin of the University of California, Los Angeles, reported that one third of those treated with antidepressants do not improve, and a significant proportion of the remainder get somewhat better but remain depressed. If antidepressants correct a chemical imbalance that underlies depression, all or most depressed people should get better after taking them. That they do not suggests that we have only barely begun to understand the disorder at a molecular level. As a result, we must consider other, nonchemical leads.

This Is Your Brain on Depression

A possible clue lies in brain structures. Imaging studies have revealed that certain brain areas differ in size between depressed and mentally healthy individuals. For example, the amygdala, which responds to the emotional significance of events, tends to be smaller in depressed people than in those without the disorder. Other emotional regulatory centers that appear to be reduced in volume are the hippocampus, an interior brain region involved in emotional memory, the anterior cingulate cortex, which helps to govern impulse control and empathy, and certain sections of the prefrontal cortex, which plays an important role in emotional regulation. Nevertheless, the effects of these shrinkages on depression, if any, remain an open question.

Neuroimaging studies have revealed that the amygdala, hypothalamus and anterior cingulate cortex are often less active in depressed people. Some parts of the prefrontal cortex also show diminished activity, whereas other regions display the opposite pattern. The subcallosal cingulate gyrus, a region near the anterior cingulate, often shows abnormal activity levels in depressed individuals. These differences may contribute to depression, but if they do, scientists are not sure how.

In 2012 neurosurgeon Andres M. Lozano of the University of Toronto and his associates studied the effects of deep brain stimulation of the subcallosal cingulate gyrus in depressed patients who had not benefited from standard treatments. The intervention led to a significant reduction in symptoms of depression, supporting the idea that a dysfunction in this brain area may be involved in the illness.

Findings also point to a crucial role for psychosocial factors such as stress, especially when it arises from a loss of someone close to you or a failure to meet a major life goal. When someone is under a good deal of stress, a hormone called cortisol is released into the bloodstream by the adrenal glands. Over the short term, cortisol helps humans cope with dangers by mobilizing energy stores for flight or fight. But chronically high cortisol levels can harm some bodily systems. For example, at least in animals, excess cortisol reduces the volume of the hippocampus, which in turn may contribute to depression. Despite such data, we still do not know if stress alters the human brain in ways that can lead to depression.

Seeing the Elephant

Throughout this column, we have described associations between various brain changes and depression. We have not talked about "causes," because no studies have established a cause-and-effect relation between any brain or psychosocial dysfunction and the disorder. In addition, depression almost certainly does not result from just one change in the brain or environmental factor. A focus on one piece of the depression puzzle–be it brain chemistry, neural networks or stress–is shortsighted.

The tunnel-vision approach is reminiscent of a classic story in which a group of blind men touch an elephant to learn what the animal looks like. Each one feels a different part, such as the trunk or the tusk. The men then compare notes and learn that they are in complete disagreement about the animal's appearance. To understand the causes of depression, we have to see the entire elephant–that is, we must integrate what we know at multiple scales, from molecules to the mind to the world we live in.

Referenced

The "Chemical Imbalance" Explanation for Depression: Origins, Lay Endorsement, and Clinical Implications. Christopher M. France et al. in *Professional Psychology: Research and Practice*, Vol. 38, No. 4, pages 411–420; August 2007.

A Multicenter Pilot Study of Subcallosal Cingulate Area Deep Brain Stimulation for Treatment-Resistant Depression. Andres M. Lozano et al. in *Journal of Neurosurgery*, Vol. 116, No. 2, pages 315–322; February 2012.

About the Authors

Hal Arkowitz and Scott O. Lilienfeld serve on the board of advisers for Scientific American Mind. *Arkowitz is an associate professor of psychology at the University of Arizona, and Lilienfeld is a psychology professor at Emory University.* *The authors wish to thank Francisco Moreno and Alfred Kaszniak for their invaluable comments.*

Is Chronic Anxiety a Learning Disorder?

By Daniel Barron

Lisa Barlow, whose name I have changed to protect her privacy, is at her kitchen table in Washington DC when she realizes that each Sunday, fifteen passenger trains depart for New Haven, CT. She's a successful copy editor and has a meeting in New Haven early Monday morning. She has no plans Sunday, so doesn't care when she arrives or how long it takes. She travels coach so has thirty tickets to choose from: fifteen departures each with two price options.

Should she choose the more-expensive flexible ticket over the locked-in value ticket? Does she want to leave earlier or later? Brunch in DC or lunch in New Haven? She can't decide.

She scrolls the screen up and down, up and down, faster and faster. Her eyes dart about the webpage. She feels a rising tension in her chest. Her breathing shortens. Her thoughts race in and out of her mind like the breath in her lungs. She touches her face and notices the telltale sign: it's numb. She reaches into her pocket, where she safeguards a small pill for moments like these. A pharmacologic reset button.

Barlow has had panic attacks since High School–the first over a social drama, the second after her science teacher told her that if she refused to dissect a pig, she'd amount to nothing. She suspects her attacks have something to do with her parents, whose difficult marriage often forced her to choose between them. This, a therapist explained, was an "impossible choice," one with permanent consequences yet no clear answer. Now as an adult, when faced with a decision that has no clear answer–even something as simple as booking a train ticket–her brain is programmed to panic.

Barlow is a capable and confident professional whose job it is to make hundreds of decisions each day. Why couldn't she see the difference between which parent to be with and what train to take? There must have been something else going on.

Anxiety as a Learning Problem

Michael Browning is a practicing psychiatrist who directs Oxford's Computational Psychiatry laboratory. I met Browning as a fourth year medical student. I'd taken a break from Yale to work for six months at Warneford Hospital, a beautiful limestone building from 1826. Browning's latest paper, *Anxious individuals have difficulty learning the causal statistics of aversive environments*, had been published in *Nature Neuroscience* just months before I arrived and I was excited to learn cutting-edge neuroscience in the city of dreaming spires.

Browning is a pleasant-looking fellow—normal height, normal build, balding (which I personally hope is normal). My first day, Browning walked me around the lab, introducing me to the other graduate students and post-docs. "This is Daniel Barron, he's come here from some university in the U.S. to work on some sort of project," he would say in his Scottish accent with a flat expression. He showed me where the "bog" (bathroom) was, where we had tea, where I could put my cowboy boots and hat if, as a Texan, I felt inclined to wear them on a rainy day.

Although Browning enjoyed cardiology and nephrology as a medical student, he became a computational psychiatrist because he found mental illnesses more compelling. Cardiologists treat the heart like a pump and they measure and calculate how well the pump is working. Nephrologists treat the kidney like a filter and measure and calculate how well the filter is working. Psychiatrists don't really know how to view the brain. And we don't know how to measure or calculate how well the brain is working. This is what Browning wants to do.

After his psychiatry residency, Browning began treating patients with major depression and bipolar disorder and noticed how extremely common anxiety is in these patients. Knowing someone has a cognitive symptom—like a panic attack when booking a train ticket—is clinically useful because it suggests a treatment goal (i.e. book tickets without panicking), something to target with clinical interventions like cognitive behavioral therapy (CBT).

CBT helps patients learn to look at anxiety-provoking situations in a new, less threating way. That you can successfully treat anxiety with CBT indicates that CBT is helpful. But on a more fundamental level, it also indicates that patients can *learn* how to not be anxious. Browning also noted that, reversing this logic, it also means that anxiety involves a learning process gone awry.

Learning on the (Coffee) Run

Measuring how we learn is hard. Experimentally, we can observe people's behavior; e.g. did someone answer a question correctly? Or did they complete a task as they were taught? This treats the brain like a black box, wherein cognitive "stuff" happens and decisions magically appear.

Learning theory provides a way to peer into this black box with mathematics. Learning theory describes how the brain builds models of the world, with the goal of understanding how to behave. According to learning theory, people develop models about the world based on the outcomes of their actions ("I did X and Y happened, so X gives me Y").

Imagine that one afternoon, you want a really good cup of coffee. To get it, you need to walk to one of two nearby coffee shops: one is an international chain, the other is run by some local hipsters. The chain coffee shop has a lot going for it: there's a standard menu; the coffee is made nearly the same way every time; the same music plays at corporate-specified volume; the wifi always works. The last time you went, you left with a fairly good cup of coffee and so, in learning theory terms, we'd say this coffee run ended with only a small prediction error, meaning what you expected is roughly what you got. If someone asked you how often this happens, you'd give a ballpark 75% of the time because you feel that overall the chain store is a pretty stable, safe bet even if you don't always leave with a really good cup of coffee.

Now consider the hipster coffee shop: the seasonal menu is locally sourced so your favorite made-from-scratch pastry may or may not be available; rotating "coffee artists" put their own spin on every drink; sometimes there's jazz, sometimes heavy metal; sometimes the wifi works, often it doesn't. When the stars align, you have the absolute best coffee experience. But because every few weeks the hipsters change things up, you often leave with no pastry and whatever Lars felt like making you. This leads to a large prediction error and, crucially, you're never quite sure what to expect. From a learning theory perspective the hipster coffee shop is a volatile environment.

Now imagine that you have three consecutive bad experiences at both places: where do you go next? Because the chain store has a 75% overall likelihood of being pretty good, those three strikes don't affect your belief in the chain store that much and you're likely to go back. But the hipster coffee shop is more volatile, so after three strikes, you could decide that the place has gone to shit and ne'er return.

In both cases there was a prediction error (although you expected a good cup of coffee, you got a bad one three times), but because the hipster coffee shop is a more volatile place, you weighed the new information more heavily and *learned* from it more in terms of your overall belief. How much prediction errors sculpt your belief is called the learning rate. Your learning rate for each coffee shop depends on the volatility.

The Brain as a Learning Machine

When he started at Oxford, Browning was keen to measure how people learn. Timothy Behrens and several colleagues had recently designed a reward game wherein participants tried to win a pot of money. To get this money, they had to click on a green or blue rectangle, which would inch them closer (or not) to that money. Because it was unclear which rectangle (blue or green) they needed to choose, players learned which was more likely to lead to a reward by trial and error, while playing the game. Like learning which coffee shop to go to by frequenting different coffee shops multiple times.

Also similar to the coffee shop analogy, Behrens developed two versions of the game: a stable version where blue rectangles led to a reward 75% of the time and a volatile version wherein the reward sometimes followed blue, sometimes green. Everyone played both versions of the game, allowing Behrens to see how quickly they could learn each version.

To win, people would have to mentally model how volatile the game was at any point in time. Behrens wanted to see how well the human brain stacked up to an "ideal learner", or a computer trained to make the winning decision at every step. That seemed like a lot of computational heavy-lifting.

But Behrens discovered–quite surprisingly–that people performed quite well, on par with the ideal learner. Behrens also discovered that he could measure how people played the game differently, depending on how volatile the task was. As the game switched from the steady, 75% version to the more volatile version, people adjusted their learning rate in a mathematically-rigorous way. Human brains could actually *compute* how chain coffee shops differed from hipster coffee shops.

Behrens had created a scenario that allowed him to treat the brain as a decision-making machine. By measuring how someone played his game, Behrens could tell whether someone's brain was working ideally.

Of course, Browning's patient's brains weren't working ideally. They were anxious. Since he suspected that anxiety was related to learning, he wondered whether he could use Behren's game to measure where and how his patient's decision-making machine had broken down.

Measuring is Complex

Browning wanted a measure of how people learn; something tidy that he could discuss with a patient: "Mrs. Robinson, we're concerned about your learning rate."

During my medicine rotations, I remember screening patients for known causes of pump malfunction, risk factors of heart disease like hypertension, cholesterol and smoking. There was something deeply triumphant about telling a patient, "you have a low risk of heart disease," as if we had together avoided catastrophe. This idea of whittling down heart disease to three risk factors is a classic reductionist overture. And it is, by design, a deceit.

Heart disease is complex and, of course, can't be completely explained by hypertension, cholesterol, and smoking. In fact, we don't (and might never) understand *everything* about *everyone's* heart disease–genes, exercise, stress from work or love, something in the water, and so on could each play some crucial yet-undefined role. Without question, looking at only three risk factors misrepresents the complexity of heart disease–but, studies have shown that it is a *useful* simplification.

Clinicians seem comfortable reducing heart disease to three risk factors–we are, after all, only talking about a pump. But we tend to cringe when we consider our inner lives, our own emotions and mental states through the same reductionist lens.

Imagine that you're Barlow's psychiatrist. She comes to your office not long after refusing to dissect the pig. She's shaken and buries her face in her hands crying, "what if I amount to nothing!" You learn about her childhood, her impossible choice between parents. You connect with her, you empathize with her, you want to help.

Now consider your next step: are you going to ask her to sit in front of a computer and click on blue and green rectangles to win a pot of fake money? How much confidence would you have in such a clinical measure? Do you think you could persuade Barlow that her learning rate as measured by the box game has much bearing on her anxiety?

I'd question my devotion to reductionism here too. The box game seems too abstract and too removed from the raw, clinical realities of panic.

But recall that cardiologists once felt this way–the connection between heart attacks, blood pressure and cholesterol isn't obvious. The very existence of blood pressure wasn't obvious–even though people had seen blood spurting out of people's veins for millennia, no one thought to *measure* blood pressure until the 18th century.

Three hundred years ago, people would have occasional chest pain and then, one day, just drop dead. I wonder what it was like going to a doctor three hundred years ago, worried about this weird, occasional pain you have in your chest. I imagine the doctor would have traced your history: "Tell me more about your pain." Maybe during this conversation, the doctor would place leeches on your arm to "clean" your blood, maybe he would even cut your arm to get rid of "extra" blood. Without other tools or interventions, your visit was primarily a conversation; a good clinician was probably a good conversationalist. The advent of the stethoscope and sphygmomanometer–both of which require the patient and clinician to be silent–nudged this relationship from dialogue towards data. Perhaps we lost something in that silence: that subtle and artful conversation that took place while the doctor was attaching leeches to your forearm.

Cardiologists didn't become useful because they thought of cleverer questions to ask their patients, but because they developed tools to reduce complex diseases to things they could measure and study and treat.

Simply figuring out that death had *causes*–that it wasn't simply the Fates or Wheel of Fortune–was itself a monumental intellectual leap. Careful investigation reduced death to specific causes like heart attacks caused by heart disease. And it was only decades-long studies of thousands of patients (e.g the Framingham Heart Study) that helped us reduce heart disease from vague, subjective symptoms to specific, measurable risk factors. Data made us comfortable with reductionism because data led us to solutions that matter.

So Browning wants to gather data because he wants to reduce anxiety to a useful measure. Yet reductionism comes at a price. In Barlow's case, the price might be losing a lot of what is real: her stories. To measure anxiety, we might jettison the richness and complexity of Barlow's interaction with her mother. But maybe this richness isn't as important as we'd like to believe. No one seems to long for the golden age of "leeching conversation."

An Anxious Machine

While Behren's experiment was underway, Browning had begun to work with Sonia Bishop, a computational neuroscientist also at Oxford. Bishop was keen to measure how anxiety affects learning, specifically how anxious people think about future negative events.

Together, they modified Behrens's reward game–instead of winning money for choosing the correct rectangle, you'd get an electric zap if you choose incorrectly. To see how volatility affected learning rate, they occasionally changed the likelihood of getting shocked. They called this an "aversive learning task" and used it to measure how people with varying levels of anxiety navigate unsavory situations.

They discovered that, like Behren's original study, non-anxious people could sense when the game was more volatile and adapt their strategy like an "ideal learner"–the more stable the task, the less an unexpected zap affected their beliefs about future events. But the more anxious a person was, the less they recognized and adapted their learning rate during the volatile game. Anxious people, it seemed, were unable to recognize and learn from volatility (which makes me wonder whether hipster coffee shops collect anxious customers).

In their *Nature Neuroscience* paper, Browning and his colleagues wondered whether being cognitively blind to volatility could make the world seem less predictable and negative outcomes less avoidable–perhaps like seeing every unclear decision as one of Barlow's impossible choices? This in turn might further reinforce someone's overall level of anxiety, creating a spiral into deepening anxiety and other mental illnesses like depression.

While Browning's study needs to be extended and replicated, the proposed relationship between volatility and learning rate has clear clinical implications. It reduces clinical focus from cognitive symptoms (e.g. to dissect or not dissect a pig?), to a specific, measurable process that has gone awry. And instead of treating someone's fear of pig dissection (which is simply one instantiation of an underlying "impossible choice" problem), clinicians could measure how well people perceive and learn from volatility and how this changes with treatment.

The Fire

"So I had a house fire two weeks ago," Barlow told me when I asked whether previous therapists had measured her anxiety, maybe with clinical symptom scales. Two days before the end of a four month kitchen remodel, her contractor had left a couple of oily rags on the floor. Overnight, some varnish cured and the rags burst into flames. "I lost a bunch of stuff–I probably have those scales, but they might have been ruined."

"Wait. I'm sorry, what?" I said, taken aback that, after speaking for nearly an hour about her emotional highs and lows, Barlow somehow forgot to tell me that her house had recently caught fire. The same person who was paralyzed by the prospect of buying a train ticket was taking an apartment fire in stride.

"The real damage was from the water and smoke," she mentioned coolly, "the fire department kind of power washed my apartment." As she talked, I thought of my own kitchen remodel last year–choosing from the seemingly infinite types of cabinets, knobs, and light fixtures, etc. An impossible number of choices. I mentioned this mountain of decisions and she laughed, "I had a hard time picking out the paint color for the walls and now, I might have to choose where the walls go. But really, no I don't think I have those measures," she said, shifting seamlessly back from catastrophe to clinical scales.

Barlow said her therapists typically just ask whether she was *feeling* better, a question that I often ask my own patients. Every time I do, I'm a bit annoyed with myself–someone with heart disease might walk up a steep flight of stairs and feel a dull pain in their chest, but they certainly wouldn't feel how much cholesterol was in their blood or how narrow their coronary arteries had become. Clinical tests exist because symptoms rarely reflect the underlying disease process, which is often invisible to us.

Like cholesterol or blood pressure, Browning reminded me that learning rate presents a potential therapeutic target. One could imagine a CBT intervention aimed at helping anxious people better understand volatility in a shifting environment. Or perhaps a medication could modify the brain's inherent learning rate, allowing someone to better separate "impossible choices" from simple errands. But also like cholesterol or blood pressure, learning rate captures something invisible and unintuitive, something that we'd never see or include in our clinical decision without a tool to measure it.

Perhaps Browning is on to something. Perhaps measuring learning rate could benefit clinical practice. I'm hopeful, but if the history of measuring and treating heart disease is any indication, finding tidy measures of anxiety will take large, collaborative efforts over many years. Measurements of learning are still in the experimental stage, so it's best to maintain a healthy skepticism, to have a healthy learning rate. "There's a lot of promise," Browning cautioned, "What there isn't is a lot of data." Hopefully, we'll have a better answer in a few years.

The views expressed are those of the author(s) and are not necessarily those of Scientific American.

About the Author

Daniel Barron is incoming Medical Director of the Interventional Pain Psychiatry Program at Brigham and Women's Hospital, a research clinic devoted to developing better tools to define pain and psychiatric conditions. He completed his medical training and psychiatry residency at Yale University and his fellowship in pain medicine at the University of Washington. He the author of Reading Our Minds: The Rise of Big Data Psychiatry. *Follow him on Twitter @daniel__barron or visit him at danielsbarron.com.*

Faulty Circuits

By Thomas R. Insel

In most areas of medicine, doctors have historically tried to glean something about the underlying cause of a patient's illness before figuring out a treatment that addresses the source of the problem. When it came to mental or behavioral disorders in the past, however, no physical cause was detectable so the problem was long assumed by doctors to be solely "mental," and psychological therapies followed suit.

Today scientific approaches based on modern biology, neuroscience and genomics are replacing nearly a century of purely psychological theories, yielding new approaches to the treatment of mental illnesses.

Many illnesses previously defined as "mental" are now recognized to have a biological cause: in autism, for example, it is an abnormality in the connections between neurons, often attributable to genetic mutations; schizophrenia is now viewed and treated as a developmental brain disorder. Yet the public and even clinicians have had difficulty accepting that certain other mental disorders such as depression, obsessive-compulsive disorder (OCD) or post-traumatic stress disorder (PTSD) could also be physiological disorders of the brain.

A primary reason that the understanding of such mental disorders has lagged so far behind other areas of medicine is that unlike classical neurological illnesses such as Parkinson's disease or the aftermath of a stroke, where the damage is visible, mental disorders are not marked by conspicuous lesions in the brain–a physical cause is still not obvious. The newest imaging technologies for mapping function in the living brain, though, allow the detection of problems with activity levels in, or communication between, brain areas, even when there is no observable loss of cells.

Neuroimaging has opened up the black box of the brain so that mental disorders can, for the first time, be studied as abnormalities in the connections between distant areas of the brain or, in some cases, problems in the coordination of brain areas whose activity is normally synchronized. Brain regions that function together to carry out normal mental operations can be thought of as analogous to electrical circuits. And the latest research shows that the malfunctioning of entire circuits may underlie many mental disorders.

The details of each disorder's "circuit diagram" or map are still emerging. But this new view is already producing seismic shifts in psychiatry, opening avenues to more empirical diagnosis of mental illnesses and providing insights into their underlying causes, which promises more effective forms of treatment.

Stuck in Overdrive?

Depression offers perhaps the best example of the rapid progress being made in understanding the biology of mental illness. Major depressive disorder, the official diagnostic term for depression, affects 16 percent of all Americans, potentially leading to loss of work, substance abuse and suicide. It is also one of the most prevalent illnesses in the developed world, where it is the leading cause of medical disability among people between the ages of 15 and 44. The symptoms include not only a profound sense of despair with helplessness and hopelessness but also a range of physical symptoms such as loss of appetite, sleep disturbances, constipation and fatigue that is sometimes mixed with agitation. Depression is known to disturb the immune system and multiple hormonal systems and to increase one's risk for cardiovascular disease. Yet despite its widespread effects on the body, depression is fundamentally a brain disorder. And considerable evidence points to a tiny region in the brain's prefrontal cortex (PFC) called area 25 as a hub for the circuitry underlying depression.

The designation "area 25" comes from a German neurologist, Korbinian Brodmann, who assigned numbers to various regions of the cortex in his classic 1909 atlas of the human brain. For the past 100 years this hard-to-reach region, which sits deep in the midline at the front of the brain, has garnered little attention. But over the past decade discovery of its critical role in depression has turned area 25 into high-interest real estate among clinical neuroscientists. Helen Mayberg and her colleagues at Emory University, for example, have shown that the region is overly active in depression and that symptom improvement after virtually all forms of treatment, from medication to psychotherapy, is accompanied by decreased activity in this same region.

Other clues also point to area 25 as having a pivotal role in depression. The region is exceptionally rich with serotonin transporters—molecules that manage the amount of the neurotransmitter serotonin available to neurons. (Many antidepressant medications are believed to act on these transporters, enhancing neural signaling through serotonin.) While at the National Institute of Mental Health, Lukas Pezawas, Andreas Meyer-Lindenberg and their colleagues studied brain scans from more than 100 nondepressed individuals to compare those with "short" and "long" variations of the serotonin transporter gene and found only a single but consistent difference in the subjects' brains. Participants with the short variation of this gene, which causes less of the transporter protein to be manufactured and is believed to confer a higher risk of depression, had reduced brain tissue volume in area 25. Moreover, in the short-variant subjects, the activity of area 25 was functionally uncoupled from that of subcortical brain regions, such as the amygdala.

As a result of this study and others, neuroscientists now think of depression as a circuitry disorder involving abnormal activity in area 25 that disrupts its vast connected network, including the hypothalamus and brain stem, which influence changes in appetite, sleep and energy; the amygdala and insula, which affect anxiety and mood; the hippocampus, which is critical to memory processing and attention; and parts of the frontal cortex, which mediate insight and self-esteem.

The brain, after all, is an information-processing organ, constantly integrating sensory inputs and coordinating responses. To extend the circuitry analogy, area 25 is believed to serve as a governor for a vast network, sensing and modulating the activity levels of other brain centers for fear, memory and self-esteem. A dysfunctional area 25 might therefore fail to coordinate the activity of these other centers so that information processing is biased, leading to distorted assessments of the internal and external world. If this conception is correct, resetting the firing of area 25 should moderate each of these downstream centers, thereby lessening the symptoms of depression. Indeed, Mayberg has demonstrated that direct electrical stimulation near area 25 reduces the activity of this node and can lead to recovery in people with depression who did not respond to standard therapies.

If area 25 can cause the brain, like a computer, to get stuck in a loop of abnormal activity, then the goal of treatment might be akin to "rebooting" a computer that has become frozen. The same principle can be applied to other mental disorders, particularly OCD, which appears even to a casual observer as though the sufferer is trapped in a cycle of abnormal thoughts and behaviors.

Relentless Repetition

In an earlier era, obsessive-compulsive disorder was considered the prototypic neurosis, caused by psychic conflict, and ideal for treatment by psychoanalysis. People with OCD suffer from intrusive, repetitive thoughts (obsessions) and may be impaired by the need to perform stereotypic, repetitive rituals (compulsions). Some people may feel they are contaminated and will wash repetitively, to the point of abrading their skin. Others have a nagging sense of having failed to carry out some responsibility and will need to check the stove or the faucets or the doorknobs repeatedly before leaving the house. While people with this condition generally realize that their thoughts are senseless, they cannot control either the obsessions or compulsions, and in severe cases they may become completely disabled.

Patients with OCD often describe their symptoms as "mental tics," as though they were physical movements that are not under voluntary control. Indeed, many people with OCD have actual tics as well as obsessive thoughts. Most neuroscientists believe the regulation of movement involves a series of loops in the brain linking the cortex with brain areas such as the basal ganglia, which are centers for initiating and coordinating various aspects of movement. The involuntary motions seen in motor tics or more dramatically in Huntington's disease reflect abnormal activity in this circuit, usually originating in the basal ganglia. Neuroimaging studies of patients with OCD have discovered abnormal activity in an adjacent loop that includes the orbitofrontal cortex, which is involved in complex tasks such as decision making, the ventral caudate nucleus within the basal ganglia, and the thalamus, which relays and integrates sensory information.

Evidence for overactivity in this circuit in OCD comes from more than just neuroimaging research. Most people with OCD report a profound reduction in symptoms with treatment, whether behavior therapy or medication, and this symptom improvement consistently goes along with a decrease in orbitofrontal cortical activity. In patients who do not respond to medication or behavior therapy, actually disconnecting the orbitofrontal cortex from the caudate either by cutting the axons, or nerve fibers, that link them or by inhibiting electrical activity along the fibers also reduces the symptoms of severe OCD. Such a clear effect produced by physically altering the connections within a brain circuit offers strong evidence for the principle that symptoms of mental disorders can arise from the dysfunction of a specific circuit.

The underlying cause of the original circuit malfunction in OCD and other mental disorders is a separate question and may have complex answers. In some cases, a preexisting vulnerability may be present. Just as predispositions to high cholesterol or high blood glucose can run in families, individual genetic variations can influence the brain's development and operation. As in other complex health disorders, however, a genetic vulnerability does not produce illness alone—environment and experiences usually interact with genetic variations and may cause disease in some people but not others. This recognition that the brain's individual biology may interact with experiences to cause or exacerbate disordered circuits is particularly helpful in understanding the aftermath of trauma.

Unlearning Fear

Post-traumatic stress disorder is one of the most common afflictions of veterans returning from war. Once called combat neurosis or battle fatigue, it is now classified as an anxiety disorder that includes disturbing intrusive thoughts, such as flashbacks to a specific traumatic event, nightmares, a high state of vigilance and sleep disturbance. The disorder is also increasingly recognized in nonveterans who are victims of civilian violence such as rape or terrorism and even automobile accidents.

At first glance, PTSD seems unlikely to be a disorder caused by abnormal brain circuitry. Even its name describes the "cause" as an external event–a specific trauma. Symptoms such as disturbed sleep and increased vigilance are to be expected immediately after a traumatic experience, and for most people they naturally fade with time. PTSD, however, develops weeks and months later in about 20 percent of trauma victims. They continue to experience acute stress responses–in essence, intense fear reactions–to memories or other cues evocative of the original trauma.

In psychotherapy, the process of reducing fear is called extinction. It means specifically that through repeated exposure to a particular trauma-related memory or cue, without adverse consequences, a patient is able to sever that cue from an automatic extreme fear response and to learn a new, neutral response to it. PTSD can thus be considered a failure of extinction. And recovery, whether natural or through therapy, requires new learning. Recent evidence from studies of animals and of people suggests that a dysfunctional circuit may make extinction harder to achieve, leaving a person vulnerable to developing PTSD.

The key hubs in the brain for fear are the amygdala and an adjacent galaxy of cells called the bed nucleus of the stria terminalis.

These regions drive virtually all the symptoms of fear: racing heart, increased sweating, freezing and exaggerated startle responses. Nerve cells in the amygdala project their long, slender axons to centers in the brain stem that control those autonomic functions and also to areas in the forebrain that influence motivation, decision making, and the saliency of specific stimuli. But if the amygdala is the engine of fear, something in the brain should be responsible for turning it off when conditions change and fear is no longer necessary or appropriate.

Studies by Greg Quirk and his colleagues at the University of Puerto Rico show that a tiny area within the prefrontal cortex of rodents, known as the infralimbic region, is central to fear extinction. After teaching the animals to be afraid of a certain stimulus and then using extinction training so the animals could overcome their fear, Quirk's group found that activity in the infralimbic area increases during extinction, serving as a brake on the amygdala. Experimental microstimulation of cells in the infralimbic appears to cause extinction behavior, even in animals that have not been trained to overcome their fear. Furthermore, blocking neural function in this tiny prefrontal region impairs extinction in animals that have been trained, suggesting that the activity of this brain region is both necessary and sufficient to overcome fear.

In PTSD sufferers, neuroimaging studies point to abnormal activity in the ventromedial prefrontal cortex (vmPFC), which is comparable to the rat's infralimbic region. Five different studies have found that when exposed to trauma-related cues, people with PTSD show reduced activity in the vmPFC. They also have a smaller vmPFC relative to trauma-exposed control subjects without PTSD. Indeed, Mohammed Milad and his colleagues at Massachusetts General Hospital in a study of healthy volunteers recently reported that the thickness of this region was correlated directly with the capacity to extinguish fear memories. Elizabeth Phelps and her colleagues at New York University have demonstrated that extinction learning in humans, just as in rodents, involves an increase in vmPFC activity and a decrease in amygdala activity.

Neuroimaging has begun to identify the biological basis for improvements through cognitive-behavioral therapy, a form of talk therapy that emphasizes changing a patient's responses to difficult situations. The imaging shows the importance of the hippocampus for assessing context and of the dorsolateral prefrontal cortex for learning to tolerate and overcome fear. Because the dorsolateral prefrontal cortex does not connect directly to the amygdala, however, the vmPFC is thought to be the critical link between them that allows cognitive treatment to produce new learning and recovery.

Fundamental Shifts

The examples I have described from studies of people with depression, OCD and PTSD all suggest a correlation between the activity of interconnected regions of the brain and the abnormal behavior and feelings that characterize those disorders. In each case, the prefrontal cortex is involved, which is not surprising. The PFC is a brain region that is less developed in other mammals, which makes it difficult to study in laboratory animals but also suggests that it is central to what makes us human. Scientists' best estimation is that the PFC acts as an overall governor for the brain and is the place where our most complex goals and motivations are processed so that we can make decisions and plan for the future.

In each of the disorders described, though, a different PFC structure and different connected regions appear to be involved. Beyond these examples, abnormal activity has also been seen in the dorsolateral prefrontal cortex in schizophrenia, and delayed maturation of the entire PFC between the ages of seven and 12 has been seen in attention-deficit hyperactivity disorder.

Although these correlations are compelling, further research is required to establish precisely which aspects of brain activity underlie these and other mental disorders. Data about genes that may increase risk for a given disorder will also help unravel the physiological mechanisms involved.

An ability to identify the brain circuit malfunctions underlying mental illness could have broad implications for diagnosis and treatment. At present, mental disorders are classified by their symptoms, which may overlap in many conditions and are not linked to any particular biological evidence. Reclassifying disorders based on brain function could yield a system of diagnosis based on biomarkers–biological signs such as brain activity patterns or chemical or structural changes specific to the condition. Just as blood tests of cholesterol or prostate-specific antigen levels and physiological measures such as electrophysiology and imaging scans are used in the rest of medicine, mental disorders could be diagnosed with greater precision and possibly identified earlier by their distinctive biological markers.

Currently a defining criterion for diagnosing schizophrenia is an episode of psychosis, just as heart disease was once defined by a person having suffered a heart attack. For brain disorders, behavioral and cognitive symptoms may be late manifestations of dysfunction in a circuit, and symptoms may appear only after compensatory mechanisms no longer suffice. In Parkinson's, observable symptoms emerge only after 80 percent of the dopamine-producing cells in the substantia nigra deteriorate. In Huntington's, motor problems become evident after 50 percent of basal ganglia neurons are lost.

Interventions will depend on the nature of the disorder. Studies of circuit functioning have shown not only that certain treatments such as cognitive-behavioral therapy work but how they may work by altering brain activity, and these insights might be used to improve existing therapy techniques. Many current antidepressant and antipsychotic medications are also effective, but no more so than the drugs available 40 years ago. A better understanding of the physiological malfunctions in the brain underlying depression will likely lead to more targeted and curative treatments.

Perhaps the most immediate result of approaching mental disorders as brain circuit disorders will be changing public perception of these illnesses. In different generations, people with mental illness have been stigmatized as possessed, dangerous, weak-willed or victimized by bad parents. Science supports none of this. A scientific approach to mental disorders could allow those who struggle with these illnesses to receive full acceptance and the high-quality care that they deserve.

From the scientific standpoint, it is difficult to find a precedent in medicine for what is beginning to happen in psychiatry. The intellectual basis of this field is shifting from one discipline, based on subjective "mental" phenomena, to another, neuroscience. Indeed, today's developing science-based understanding of mental illness very likely will revolutionize prevention and treatment and bring real and lasting relief to millions of people worldwide.

About the Author

Thomas R. Insel, a psychiatrist and neuroscientist, is director of the National Institute of Mental Health, the federal agency that supports the study of mental illnesses. His early clinical research revealed the role of serotonin in obsessive-compulsive disorder, and his animal studies of the neurobiology underlying social attachment identified the importance of brain receptors for oxytocin and other substances in forming social bonds. In describing new findings in the neurocircuitry of mood disorders, as in all his work, Insel endeavors to bridge divisions between biology and psychology by highlighting the reciprocal relations between neural activity and behavior.

Section 2: Causes of Anxiety and Depression in Today's World

News about Racial Violence Harms Black People's Mental Health

By Melba Newsome

For months, Desmond Ellington assiduously refused to watch the videotaped killing of George Floyd. When former Minneapolis police office Derek Chauvin went on trial for his murder, Ellington did not turn on the television until he saw a headline on his smartphone that the verdict would be announced within the hour. It was not that he did not care about what was happening; it was that he cared too much.

For the 37-year-old Black singer and actor, the news accounts and social media videos of racial violence and the killings of unarmed Black people that too often go unpunished were not just demoralizing, they were traumatizing. "It gets to the point where you decide, 'I have to turn off the television because I have my sanity to take care of,'" says Ellington, an Arkansas native who lives in New York. "It's like a sadness, a hopelessness. Those images just keep coming like weeds. You pick one weed, and two more sprout up. So you gonna set the whole yard on fire to kill the weeds? It wears on your psyche."

A growing body of research has documented the detrimental effects of both interpersonal and structural racism. The Centers for Disease Control and Prevention notes that centuries of racism have had a profound and negative impact on the mental and physical health of people of color. Investigators at Columbia University found that experiencing racism can result in traumatic stress linked to negative mental health outcomes, such as depression, anger and low self-esteem. The American Public Health Association calls racism a social determinant of health akin to housing, education, and employment and a barrier to health equity.

A study recently published in the *Proceedings of the National Academy of Sciences USA* adds a new layer to an understanding of the pervasive health effects of racism. Lead author David Curtis of the University of Utah and his colleagues showed that widely publicized anti-Black violence negatively affects the mental health of many Black Americans even if they do not directly experience it.

The study's authors conducted the first nationwide scientific assessment of these media reports using 49 high-profile incidents that occurred between 2013 and 2017. They included media reports of 38 police killings of Black individuals, as well as coverage of about nine legal decisions not to indict or convict officers involved in some of those killings.

Using weekly data from the Behavioral Risk Factor Surveillance System survey, the researchers assessed the mental health impacts on people during this period. Black respondents reported more poor mental health days during the time when two or more of these events happened in the country. Legal decisions not to prosecute or convict the officers involved in the killings were most clearly associated with poor mental health days, Curtis says. This reflects Black people's concern and dismay about what they see as the systemic injustice that follows a much publicized incident and the failure to hold anyone accountable more than their reaction to the initial wrong perpetrated by any single individual.

Those emotions also resonate with personal experiences in which racism is ever present. As a senior operations engineer who is starting a job at Amazon later this month, 26-year-old Adam Williams works in a field in which Black people are dramatically underrepresented. That mirrors his life on a college campus just a few years ago. When he graduated from Purdue University in 2017, just 1.6 percent of the students in the College of Engineering were Black, a statistic that figured into the way he was perceived.

Initially, none of Williams's classmates wanted to be his lab partner, and they seemed shocked when he answered questions correctly in class. "I saw Nazi propaganda scattered across campus detailing how I was genetically inferior," he says of literature disparaging Black people. "I was hastily labeled a delinquent, followed through stores, questioned by police under bogus pretenses and frequently assumed that the only way I could be at Purdue was as an athlete."

For his part, Ellington considers himself lucky to have encountered little overt and direct racism. Yet despite achieving a measure of professional success and traveling the country as a member of the cast of *Hamilton*, he cannot shake the feeling that he is just one wrong move away from becoming another statistic.

"I'm still very aware that it could happen to me," he says. "I have to know how to conduct myself when I'm out. I'm always thinking, 'Am I walking or standing too close to this person?' It's a burden that I have to be in that box so I can get back home to my family. It's so emotionally and physically draining. You don't even realize how much until you see another Black man get shot. I think it's in those moments you realize how much of a burden it is to be Black in America."

Psychologist Vanessa Volpe runs the Black Health Lab at North Carolina State University, where she studies the impact of direct and vicarious racism on physical health. She compares the kind of hypervigilance Ellington talks about–trying to navigate the thicket of structural, systemic and interpersonal racism–to driving a car with the parking brake on.

"Because exposure to racism is chronic, frequent and can happen at any time, you have to be vigilant to protect yourself," Volpe says. "Over time, your body is going to experience this wear and tear that will result in much greater rates of morbidity and earlier mortality for Black folks, compared to white people. A lot of times we think, 'Just get a better car or replace the parking brake,' but that's a Band-Aid. What can we do so that Black people don't even have that exposure in the first place?"

About the Author

Melba Newsome is an independent journalist in Charlotte, N.C., whose work has appeared in Prevention, Newsweek, Wired, Politico, Yale E 360, Oprah *and the* New York Times, *among other publications.*

Pandemic Year One Saw a Dramatic Global Rise in Anxiety and Depression

By Gary Stix

COVID has posed a threat to body—and mind—for *all people* on the planet—the essence of the Greek-rooted coupling of ϖᾶν (pan) plus δῆμος (demos) to form the now too-familiar noun.

Yet there has been no incisive examination to date of the pandemic's psychological toll on a global basis. It is difficult to determine increases in cases of depression and anxiety because of a lack of data. No good numbers exist for many countries and even whole continents (Africa and South America).

Despite gaps in the data, a team largely based at the University of Queensland in Australia has made an estimate for 2020. "This study is the first to quantify the prevalence and burden of depressive and anxiety disorders by age, sex, and location globally," the researchers wrote in the *Lancet*.

The numbers themselves are devastating. Cases for depressive and anxiety disorders last year are estimated to have increased by more than a quarter—an unusually large surge.

If the pandemic had not happened, the model used by the researchers estimated there would have been 193 million cases of major depressive disorder worldwide, whereas an estimated 246 million cases actually occurred, a 28 percent increase, or an added 53 million cases. For anxiety disorders the number of cases was anticipated at 298 million, but there may have been an actual 374 million cases—a 26 percent jump, representing an added 76 million cases.

The figures for both depression and anxiety usually remain stable from year to year. Such sharp upturns cannot be counted as routine fluctuations;"This is definitely like a shock to the system from what we are typically used to seeing when it comes to the prevalence of these disorders," says Damian Santomauro, the lead author, from the Queensland Center for Mental Health Research, School of Public Health at University of Queensland.

Women and young people were hit particularly hard. Almost 52 million of the added cases for anxiety during the first COVID year were accounted for among women, contrasted with 24 million for men. Although COVID caused more death and serious illness among older people, it was younger people who faced the greatest burdens of depression and anxiety. The category with the highest burden–the 20- to 24-year age bracket–had an estimated 1,118 added depression cases per 100,000 people, and 1,331 more per 100,000 for anxiety. "We are hoping that these findings encourage more dialogue by policy makers, governments, researchers and people considering resource allocation and planning for mental health responses," says Alize Ferrari, one of the University of Queensland researchers.

The university team succeeded in making an estimate for global levels of depressive and anxiety disorders by compensating for the data that were lacking. They did so by relying on other data put together from 48 studies conducted in Western Europe, parts of North America, Australasia and other regions that actually had mental health figures. They were able to statistically link depression and anxiety data to "COVID-19 impact indicators," infection rates by country and indicators tracking diminished population movements for 204 countries. That statistical relationship between impact indicators and mental health data, analyzed for North America and other regions, could then be used to extrapolate the missing estimates for depressive and anxiety disorders for the many countries that lacked that data. All that was needed to make the calculations was the impact indicators, which exist for almost every nation.

Maxime Taquet, an academic clinical fellow in the department of psychiatry at the University of Oxford, who was not involved with the study, praised the effort as providing the first insight into the global impact of the pandemic on mental health. The study, he says, also points to the urgent need for depression and anxiety statistics from the countries for which estimates could only be made with statistical extrapolations. "We need to be quite cautious when we interpret the findings of this study because in large areas of the world we simply don't have any data," he says. Taquet wrote a commentary for the *Lancet* about the study.

The study will continue until the pandemic ends. The data are being incorporated in the larger Global Burden of Disease study, led by the Institute for Health Metrics and Evaluation (IHME) at the University of Washington. Those numbers will surely be useful. COVID's mental health consequences are sure to linger long after any unofficial declaration that the pandemic has come to a close.

About the Author

Gary Stix is a senior editor at Scientific American.

Suicide Rates Rise in a Generation of Black Youth

By Melinda Wenner Moyer

Suicide is a devastating problem among Black youth, and researchers and mental health professionals are desperate to understand why and how best to address it. A 2018 study found, for instance, that Black children between the ages of five and 12 are about twice as likely to die by suicide as white children of the same age. The urgency to deal with the issue has only grown more acute. A new study found that suicide rates among Black children and adolescents have recently been worsening: between 2003 and 2017, suicides rose in this group, especially among Black girls, whose rate of increase was more than twice as high as that of Black boys.

In the new paper, published on September 8 in the *Journal of the American Academy of Child & Adolescent Psychiatry*, researchers extracted information from Centers of Disease Control and Prevention databases about the 1,810 Black people aged five to 17 who had died by suicide between 2003 and 2017. They found that suicides rose over time during that period among Black youth of all ages and that the biggest increases occurred among teens aged 15 to 17. More than 2.5 times as many Black boys died by suicide as Black girls, but the annual increase among girls–6.6 percent–was more than twice what it was for boys.

The findings are "deeply concerning," says Janelle Goodwill, a psychologist and social worker at the University of Chicago Crown Family School of Social Work, Policy, and Practice, who was not involved in the research. They also challenge the long-held assumption that suicide rates among young white individuals are higher than those among young Black people. The September 8 paper only analyzed data through 2017, so it lacks figures for the COVID-19 pandemic. A CDC study published in August

2020 reported that, in late June of that year, more than one quarter of young adults had contemplated suicide within the past 30 days.

Suicides among Black youth may have increased for a variety of reasons. For one thing, adverse childhood experiences are extremely high in this group, says Michael A. Lindsey, a co-author of the new study and executive director of the McSilver Institute for Poverty Policy and Research at New York University, and such experiences could be increasing. Black youth may also be experiencing more racial discrimination, which has been linked to an increased risk of suicide. And they may be traumatized by headlines about the deaths of Trayvon Martin, Michael Brown and other young Black individuals.

Psychological barriers to accessing mental health care may provide another explanation for these findings. "There's a lot of stigma related to mental health treatment that seems to persist in Black communities and families," Lindsey says, "including the propensity to want to share concerns related to one's emotional and psychological well-being with family members only—and not share it with professionals."

It is unclear why rates of suicide are increasing most among Black girls, but Lindsey notes that the discrimination and sexual violence they experience may increase the risk that they will take their own life. According to the CDC, one in eight high school girls of all races experiences sexual dating violence, compared with one in 26 high school boys. Black teen girls also appear to be at a higher risk of sexual violence than girls of other races—and such violence is a known suicide risk factor. Other research has pointed to the compounding effects of sexism and racism on Black girls and how together they might increase this group's risk of depression and anxiety, compared with that of Black boys.

Black girls also follow different trajectories when contemplating suicide than Black boys do, according to another new study published in September in *Prevention Science*. Based on results from nationally representative surveys, researchers found that high schoolers who attempted suicide impulsively, without prior suicidal ideation, were disproportionately Black and male and less likely to report feelings of sadness and hopelessness. Female high schoolers, on the other hand, were more apt to feel sad and hopeless and go through mental planning steps before their attempts.

According to Meghan Romanelli, a licensed clinical social worker at the University of Washington School of Social Work and a co-author of the *Prevention Science* paper, Black boys who attempt suicide may be less likely than others to suffer from the feelings of sadness and hopelessness that characterize depression and might fit the criteria for other diagnoses, such as post-traumatic stress disorder. If so, "it's likely that these youth are experiencing symptoms or warning signs that we aren't recognizing or picking up on," she says. They may also be less likely to tell others that they are struggling.

Another condition linked to suicide in Black youth is attention deficit hyperactivity disorder, or ADHD. In the *Journal of the American Academy of Child & Adolescent Psychiatry* study, five- to 11-year-old Black children with a diagnosis of ADHD were at a heightened risk of suicide. ADHD itself might not increase suicide risk, Lindsey says. But rather symptoms of ADHD and depression—which can include irritability and interpersonal problems—can overlap and make it hard for professionals to recognize that kids with the disorder are also depressed. "The underlying reasons for why they're irritable or angry might be missed," he notes.

The new studies have important implications for suicide prevention in Black communities. Teachers, parents and mental health professionals who engage regularly with Black youth need to be educated as to "nuanced, subtle behaviors that actually might be indicating that a child is at risk," Lindsey says. They need to learn that at-risk youth may express irritability rather than sadness as a warning sign. Physical symptoms could be important, too: Lindsey's research has shown that depressed Black youth who live in low-income housing sometimes complain of physical pain. Interventions that aim to reduce the stigma associated with mental health treatment in Black communities are now becoming available. Lindsey and his colleagues developed a program called the Making

Connections Intervention to provide depressed young people with mental health care and reduce the stigma associated with receiving it.

Another goal of such interventions should be to convey the message to Black children and teenagers that they are valued members of society. Right now there is a "lack of compassion and care for young Black lives," Goodwill says, which may be fueling feelings of worthlessness. We must counteract this pernicious message, she says, so that young Black people in America understand that "their lives are full of meaning and purpose."

If You Need Help

If you or someone you know is struggling or having thoughts of suicide, help is available. Call, text, or online chat 988 to be connected to a trained crisis counselor available 24/7 through the 988 Suicide & Crisis Lifeline. This new three-digit Lifeline became active in July 2022 and was formerly the National Suicide Prevention Lifeline. The old Lifeline number remains available by calling 1-800-273-TALK (8255).

About the Author

Melinda Wenner Moyer, a contributing editor at Scientific American, *is author of* How to Raise Kids Who Aren't Assholes: Science-Based Strategies for Better Parenting–From Tots to Teens *(G. P. Putnam & Sons, 2021).*

Climate Anxiety and Mental Illness

By Brian Barnett, Amit Anand

In mid-September, with much of the American West engulfed in flames, the National Oceanic and Atmospheric Administration announced that the Northern Hemisphere just experienced its hottest summer on record. Reports like this are increasingly common, and with each one climate change continues to morph from a vague notion of far-off future catastrophe to an unsettling reality unfolding before our eyes. While denial continues to hinder efforts to respond to climate change, nearly three fourths of Americans now think it's occurring, more than 60 percent believe it is caused by humans, and more than two thirds report they're at least "somewhat worried" by it.

Recently the term "climate anxiety" has crept into the lexicon to better describe our growing concerns about climate change. While there is evidence that climate anxiety can be identified and reliably measured, what's less clear is how it relates to mental illness. Mental health providers across the world are noting the presence of climate anxiety in their patients; however, the degree to which it is influencing mental illness is not yet clear, though evidence addressing this question is slowly growing.

For years now, mental health clinicians have seen climate anxiety influencing presentations of mental illness in a variety of ways, some extreme. For example, one case reported in the medical literature discusses a 17-year-old patient who was so concerned about climate change that he became delusional, believing that if he continued to drink water or use it for tasks at home, millions of people would soon die as a result of his consumption of their water supplies. Similarly, a study of individuals with obsessive compulsive disorder found that nearly a third of individuals with OCD in Australia had compulsions focused on checking light switches, water taps, stoves and other items to reduce their carbon footprint.

Recent studies are starting to look at links between climate anxiety and mental illness in larger samples to help better understand the directionality of their relationship. In a U.S. survey of more than 340 people published in 2018, climate concerns were associated with depressive symptoms. Ecological coping, which includes proenvironmental behaviors such as reducing energy consumption, appeared to be protective against depression, indicating climate concerns and poor coping skills to address them could be causing depressive symptoms. In Tuvalu, an island country in the Pacific Ocean at significant risk of being devastated by climate change in the near future, a survey published this year found that 87 percent of respondents reported such severe climate anxiety it impaired their ability to perform at least one activity of daily living. Such high rates of debilitating distress in this group suggest that individual populations will likely see more mental illness stemming from concerns about climate change as its repercussions draw nearer to them.

So who might be more vulnerable to mental illness secondary to the uncertainties around climate change? Unsurprisingly, climate anxiety appears higher in individuals with more concern about environmental issues at baseline and those already experiencing direct effects of climate change. Climatologists also face increased risk given their in-depth knowledge on the issue coupled with the frustrating task of trying to convey it to individuals and governments that often deny or downplay it. People with high levels of neuroticism, a personality trait that increases susceptibility to mental illness, are also likely to be at high risk.

Young people are a demographic of particular concern, since a recent national survey revealed that climate changes makes 57 percent of American teens feel afraid and 43 percent hopeless. There is an extensive generational gap in climate change concern, with younger individuals being more likely to believe climate change will pose a serious threat in their lifetimes. Young people also report more functional impairment secondary to climate anxiety than older people.

As younger people embrace with growing certainty the likelihood they could be inheriting a dying planet, many are so concerned they're considering not having children in order to reduce their carbon footprint. Their worries are especially alarming in light of growing suicide rates among adolescents and young adults, with a tripling of the rate among people aged 10–14 during 2007–2017. We don't know whether climate anxiety might be affecting suicide rates in this demographic, but the possibility of a connection demands ongoing vigilance and investigation.

The sociologist Émile Durkheim, who published the first extensive study of suicide in 1897, posited that many suicides happen when free-thinking individuals feel disconnected from society and there's a weakening of a society's regulatory institutions. Our current politically fueled controversy over climate change seems to present a perfect storm for increased suicidality as American youth grow distant from a society run by older political leaders, many of whom deny climate change altogether and even seek to weaken the scientific institutions whose very job it is to bring attention to it.

They've also seen activists from their ranks such as Greta Thunberg dismissed and even personally attacked by prominent leaders, demonstrating their concerns are being ignored outright. Climate anxiety among young people is likely greatly magnified by such behavior, given the sense of powerlessness it instills.

Some individuals report adaptive responses to climate anxiety like adopting proenvironmental behaviors and participating in collective action, while others are unable to respond behaviorally at all. It's not yet apparent how these varying reactions manifest on a population level and how they're influencing humanity's response to climate change. However, a recent survey of nearly 200 people found that, while climate anxiety was associated with an emotional response to climate change, it was not correlated with a behavioral response.

If this is true for humanity as a whole, we must urgently help motivate the anxious among us. Doing so successfully will require many approaches, such as delivering cognitive-behavioral therapy to the most severely affected to demonstrating to entire populations that change is possible by better publicizing productive efforts by organizations to reduce their carbon footprints. We can't let climate anxiety stop us from responding to climate change, because now, more than ever, we need action, not paralysis.

About the Authors

Brian Barnett, M.D., is a psychiatrist at Cleveland Clinic.

Amit Anand, M.D., is a psychiatrist at Cleveland Clinic.

The Personality Trait 'Intolerance of Uncertainty' Causes Anguish during COVID

By Francine Russo

Anxiety disorders are the most common type of mental disorders in the U.S. But a simple diagnosis of generalized anxiety disorder may not capture the specifics of what bothers some people. A subgroup of anxiety sufferers may experience extreme distress when confronting the inherent uncertainties that turn up in any life circumstance, whether helping a relative with a severe illness or choosing a new route to work that is safe and easy to navigate.

Such people may respond to their feelings by leaving nothing to chance. At work, they appear polished and prepared when giving a presentation because they consider every question that could be posed by colleagues beforehand and memorize possible answers in the days leading up to a meeting. Still, all of the prep work may do little to relieve feelings of painful anxiety.

Psychologists, though, are learning new ways to treat these sufferers, who can be identified through their answers to a psychological measurement known as the intolerance of uncertainty scale (IUS). Patients can then benefit from specialized treatment.

These patients are typical of the ones psychologist Keith Bredemeier sees at the University of Pennsylvania's Center for the Treatment and Study of Anxiety. When encountering patients with a high score on the IUS, Bredemeier may explicitly target enhancing their comfort levels with life's unpredictability as a treatment goal. Since therapy is adapted to patients' salient personality traits, treatment for uncertainty distress may be added to their treatment plans just as treatments for eating disorders, for example, may focus on clients' perfectionism. And therapy for obsessive-compulsive disorder may concentrate on patients' inflated sense of responsibility.

Difficulty dealing with uncertainty was first identified in the early 1990s as a distinguishable personality trait. It is one we all have to some degree, but many of us have it at an elevated level. Like perfectionism or rigidity, it is really a predisposition, not a diagnosable disorder. People who have high levels of perfectionism, for example, are at greater risk of developing anorexia. And someone with a high level of intolerance of uncertainty (IU) may end up developing an anxiety disorder.

To cope, a person may live along a narrow, predictable track. Everything may seem fine to them on the surface, but their risk for developing anxiety, depression or emotional distress is higher—especially if something such as, say, a pandemic wreaks havoc on a carefully planned life.

In the decades since the IUS was developed, researchers have found it useful for understanding why some patients are anxious, devising targeted therapies and assessing a patient's progress. In psychology labs, investigators have probed how uncertainty affects people's brain and behavior. Clinicians have used the concept to develop programs that teach parents of autistic children strategies to help their children better tolerate uncertainty. And tourism specialists have delved into which clients might prefer guided tours instead of unguided ones. Most of all, because the pandemic blew away a sense of predictability in everyday life, the concept has sparked an explosion of research globally to find out how those who typically feel this type of distress are faring in these uncertain times and what might be done to help them.

It Began with a Hunch

In the 1990s Mark Freeston and Michel Dugas were part of a team at Laval University in Quebec looking into generalized anxiety disorder. The focus in the field was on worry. The thinking at the time "was that worry was some form of problem-solving gone wrong or a problem-solving deficit," notes Freeston, who is now at Newcastle University in England. But Freeston and his colleagues saw something different in their patients' behavior. "They knew how to solve problems, but something was getting in the way," he says. The team hypothesized that anxious people might have a negative reaction to uncertainty. Following a "clinical hunch," he says, the group developed the IUS and tested it out.

When filling out this questionnaire, people indicated how they might react to statements such as "Unforeseen events upset me greatly" and "It frustrates me not having all the information I need." The scale accurately assessed subjects' reactions–cognitive, emotional and behavioral–to uncertain situations in which they felt they did not know vital information or could not control the future.

Evolution and Fear of the Unknown

For humans and other animals, fear of uncertainty is a default state, says health psychologist Jos F. Brosschot of Leiden University in the Netherlands. Carry your cat into an unfamiliar empty room, he suggests. No fierce dog or hostile human is there, but there is also no obvious place to hide. Without a safe spot, the animal might be apt to claw at your chest in terror. "In the wild," Brosschot and his colleagues wrote in a 2018 paper, "organisms have survived not by waiting for more evidence of threat but instead by erring on the side of caution.... Those who fled at the first sign of unsafety continued to live and pass their genes."

From birth, humans have to carefully learn the cues that signal safety. For a toddler, safety is wherever their caregiver is. Over time, if we grow up in a secure environment with supportive parents, we learn to feel safe when there is no obvious danger. We become better able to tolerate uncertainty. But for those of us who grew up abused, neglected or otherwise deprived of feeling safe, uncertainty is threatening.

Uncertainty in the Lab

At the University of Reading in England, psychologist Jayne Morriss has subjected volunteers in her laboratory to unpleasant experiences that they may or may not be able to predict, from a mild electric shock to a terrifying scream. Before doing so, she already assessed them with the usual psychological tests, including the IUS. She also ascertained their thresholds for receiving a mild electric shock. Then, as they sat in front of a computer that told them whether, when or if they would receive a shock (or hear a scream), she measured their physiological responses with a magnetic resonance imaging scanner, skin conductance sensors or registers of startle response, depending on the study. Invariably, people high in IU show greater physiological distress.

One of her studies, published last year and entitled, in part, "I Told You It Was Safe," produced intriguing results. The subjects were told that they would receive a shock at a certain time, at an unknown time, or not at all—or, more emphatically, that they definitely would *not* get shocked. The surprising result is that those with high IU scores showed the greatest physiological distress during the certain-to-be-safe period.

This seems counterintuitive, yet it is easy to explain. Those of us who grew up with unpredictable danger or inconsistent safety are ever vigilant for harm. "People consistently high in IU have trouble recognizing when they are safe," Freeston says. "Just telling them it's safe isn't enough."

In fact, Morriss has shown in other studies that subjects with high IU need a greater number of exposures to a now safe scenario that was previously unsafe before they have no distress response. In other words, they have more difficulty updating their perception of safety.

Tailoring Therapy

As intolerance of uncertainty has begun to be studied as a separate trait from a tendency to worry, psychologists have identified typical behaviors—often unconstructive ones—that people use to tamp down their distress at not knowing. They overprepare, perhaps memorizing answers to all the possible questions anticipated for an upcoming presentation. Some collect every bit of information they can find online and offline. They constantly seek reassurance from others and look for media sources they can trust. Or they avoid situations with unknown outcomes. If they do not know how they will do on a test, they may avoid looking at their textbooks or procrastinate. They may impulsively make a choice, even a bad one, in order to resolve their uncertainty about something. They may also decide that they know an answer and close their minds to new information.

Bredemeier adapts treatments for these patients at his clinic. To help a client feel more comfortable with uncertainty, he first has them list situations that feel mildly to intensely uncomfortable. Let's say someone dislikes ordering from a new restaurant without first reading reviews or avoids taking a different route to work. The worst situation of all would be delegating an important task at work. The person just cannot do it.

In response, the therapist asks a client to do each task, starting with the easiest one first. A feeling of uncertainty grows, but the person stays aware of thoughts and feelings and reflects on the outcome. Maybe the client wishes they had ordered the usual takeout. Maybe they have found a favorite new restaurant. The outcome is less important than becoming more comfortable with some unpredictability. After a series of these experiments, the client is likely to score lower on IU and eventually reduce inflexible behaviors.

COVID: Uncertainty in Real Time

When the pandemic hit, none of us knew from day to day what would happen. No one knew how infections—or the threat of them—would affect work, school or travel. Nobody liked the unpredictability. Dozens of studies worldwide showed that people high in IU were at greatest risk of emotional problems.

A study published in January 2022 is especially noteworthy. Two years before COVID emerged, a team at the University of Illinois at Chicago used two methods to measure volunteers' uncertainty intolerance during predictable and unpredictable shocks. The researchers administered the IUS self-report questionnaire before the experiment. And during it, they monitored subjects' neural response with functional magnetic resonance imaging.

Two years later, at the height of the pandemic, the researchers asked these same volunteers detailed questions about their emotional reactions to the crisis. Having higher self-reported IU or greater activity in a brain area called the anterior insula during imaging independently predicted an increase in anxiety, depression or emotional distress.

Therapists have begun to target their patients' uncertainty intolerance to help them through the pandemic because COVID's unpredictability exacerbates classic IU behaviors in some people. Some read everything they can find on the Internet, wash their hands incessantly and rarely leave home. Others refuse to alter their routines even if they are putting themselves or others at risk. There are endless permutations of dealing with this continuing state of just not knowing.

As Bredemeier says, "All of us like to feel certain. It's just a question of how much distress it causes us. Intolerance of uncertainty is a matter of degree."

About the Author

Francine Russo is a journalist specializing in psychology and behavior. She is the author of Love After 50: How to Find It, Enjoy It, and Keep It *(Simon and Schuster, 2021).*

The Scientific Underpinnings and Impacts of Shame

By Annette Kämmerer

We have all felt shame at one time or another. Maybe we were teased for mispronouncing a common word or for how we looked in a bathing suit, or perhaps a loved one witnessed us telling a lie. Shame is the uncomfortable sensation we feel in the pit of our stomach when it seems we have no safe haven from the judging gaze of others. We feel small and bad about ourselves and wish we could vanish. Although shame is a universal emotion, how it affects mental health and behavior is not self-evident. Researchers have made good progress in addressing that question.

Bad For Your Health

According to philosopher Hilge Landweer of the Free University of Berlin, certain conditions must come together for someone to feel shame. Notably, the person must be aware of having transgressed a norm. He or she must also view the norm as desirable and binding because only then can the transgression make one feel truly uncomfortable. It is not even always necessary for a disapproving person to be present; we need only imagine another's judgment. Often someone will conjure an image of a parent asking, "Aren't you ashamed?" Indeed, we may internalize such admonishments so completely that the norms and expectations laid on us by our parents in childhood continue to affect us well into adulthood.

June Tangney of George Mason University has studied shame for decades. In numerous collaborations with Ronda L. Dearing of the University of Houston and others, she has found that people who have a propensity for feeling shame—a trait termed shame-proneness—often have low self-esteem (which means, conversely, that a certain degree of self-esteem may protect us from excessive feelings of shame). Tangney and Dearing are among the investigators who have found that shame-proneness can also increase one's risk for other psychological problems. The link with depression is particularly strong; for instance, one large-scale meta-analysis in which researchers examined 108 studies involving more than 22,000 subjects showed a clear connection.

In a 2009 study, Sera De Rubeis, then at the University of Toronto, and Tom Hollenstein of Queen's University in Ontario looked specifically at the trait's effects on depressive symptoms in adolescents. The project included roughly 140 volunteers between the ages of 11 and 16 and found that teenagers who exhibited greater shame-proneness were also more likely to have symptoms of depression. There also seems to be a connection between shame-proneness and anxiety disorders, such as social anxiety disorder and generalized anxiety disorder, as Thomas A. Fergus, now at Baylor University, and his colleagues reported in 2010.

Sex and Age Differences

In 2010 a team of psychologists led by Ulrich Orth of the University of Bern studied shame in more than 2,600 volunteers between the ages of 13 and 89, most of whom lived in the U.S. They found not only that men and women manifest shame differently but also that age seems to affect how readily people experience it: adolescents are most prone to this sensation; the propensity for shame decreases in middle age until about the age of 50; and later in life people again become more easily embarrassed. The authors see this pattern as a function of personality development. The identities of teenagers and young adults are not completely formed; in addition, people in this age group are expected to conform to all manner of norms that define their place in society. Uncertainty as to how to deal with these external expectations may make them quicker to feel shame. By middle age, in contrast, our character is more or less set, and norms have less impact. But as we enter old age and worry about declines in our body and our appearance, we begin to feel self-conscious again.

Guilt and Shame: Related but Different

It has been speculated that humans feel shame because it conferred some kind of evolutionary advantage on our early ancestors. For instance, it can potentially promote a group's well-being by encouraging individuals to adhere to social conventions and to work to stay in others' good graces.

Yet Tangney and others argue that shame reduces one's tendency to behave in socially constructive ways; rather it is shame's cousin, guilt, that promotes socially adaptive behavior. People often speak of shame and guilt as if they were the same, but they are not. Like shame, guilt occurs when we transgress moral, ethical or religious norms and criticize ourselves for it. The difference is that when we feel shame, we view *ourselves* in a negative light ("*I* did something terrible!"), whereas when we feel guilt, we view a particular *action* negatively ("I *did something terrible*!"). We feel guilty because our actions affected someone else, and we feel responsible.

Tangney and her co-authors explained it well in a 2005 paper: "A shame-prone individual who is reprimanded for being late to work after a night of heavy drinking might be likely to think, 'I'm such a loser; I just can't get it together,' whereas a guilt-prone individual would more likely think, 'I feel badly for showing up late. I inconvenienced my co-workers.' Feelings of shame can be painful and debilitating, affecting one's core sense of self, and may invoke a self-defeating cycle of negative affect.... In comparison, feelings of guilt, though painful, are less disabling than shame and are likely to motivate the individual in a positive direction toward reparation or change."

Further, guilt is a sign that a person can be empathetic, a trait that is important for one's ability to take someone else's perspective, to behave altruistically and to have close, caring relationships. Indeed, we can feel a sense of guilt only if we can put ourselves in another's shoes and recognize that our action caused pain or was injurious to the other person. As is generally true of young children, people who are unable to empathize cannot feel guilt.

Guilt holds us back from harming others and encourages us to form relationships for the common good. When we feel guilty, we turn our gaze outward and seek strategies to reverse the harm we have done. When we feel ashamed, we turn our attention inward, focusing mainly on the emotions roiling within us and attending less to what is going on around us.

One study that clearly associates guilt and empathy was published in 2015. Matt Treeby, then at La Trobe University in Melbourne, and his colleagues first examined the extent to which test subjects tended toward shame or guilt. Then they had the 363 participants look at facial expressions and determine whether the person was angry, sad, happy, fearful, disgusted or ashamed. Guilt-prone volunteers proved to be more accurate in their observations: they were better able to recognize the emotions of others than were shame-prone volunteers.

Of course, guilt and shame often occur together to some extent. Guilt can trigger a sense of shame in many people because of the discrepancy between the standard to which they hold themselves and the action that caused the guilt. The connection between guilt and shame grows stronger with an increase in the intentionality of our misbehavior, the number of people who witnessed it and the importance of those individuals to us. Shame will also increase if the person who was harmed by our action rejects or rebukes us.

Haunted by Original Sin

In the bible, nakedness is a source of shame. The book of Genesis 2:25 says of Adam and Eve, "And they were both naked, the man and his wife, and were not ashamed." That changed when they rebelled against God's commandment and ate of the tree of knowledge. From then on, they felt ashamed in each other's presence: "And the eyes of them both were opened, and they knew that they *were* naked; and they sewed fig leaves together, and made themselves aprons."

This biblical interpretation of nakedness as shameful still deeply informs the social norms and conventions that determine

how we deal with human physicality and sexuality. Although our notions of whether, how, where and in the presence of whom a person may be undressed have changed over the centuries, the shame we feel when we transgress the norms has remained.

Ridding oneself of guilt is often easier than overcoming shame, in part because our society offers many ways to expiate guilt-inducing offenses, including apologizing, paying fines, and serving jail time. Certain religious rituals, such as confession, may also help us deal with guilt. But shame has real staying power: it is much easier to apologize for a transgression than it is to accept oneself.

Some kinds of guilt can be as destructive as shame-proneness is–namely, "free-floating" guilt (not tied to a specific event) and guilt about events that one has no control over. In general, though, it appears that shame is often the more destructive emotion. It follows, then, that parents, teachers, judges and others who want to encourage constructive behavior in their charges would do well to avoid shaming rule-breakers, choosing instead to help them to understand the effects of their actions on others and to take steps to make up for their transgressions.

Referenced

On the Intensity of Experiencing Feelings of Shame in Mental Disorders. Annette Kämmerer in *Psychotherapie, Psychosomatik, Medizinische Psychologie*, Vol. 60, No. 7, pages 262–270; July 2010.

Tracking the Trajectory of Shame, Guilt, and Pride across the Life Span. Ulrich Orth et al. in *Journal of Personality and Social Psychology*, Vol. 99, No. 6, pages 1061–1071; December 2010.

Shame, Guilt, and Facial Emotion Processing: Initial Evidence for a Positive Relationship between Guilt-Proneness and Facial Emotion Recognition Ability. Matt S. Treeby et al. in *Cognition and Emotion*, Vol. 30, No. 8, pages 1504–1511; December 2016.

Shame and Guilt: The Good, the Bad, and the Ugly. Video lecture by June Tangney. Presented by George Mason University and ResearchChannel: https://youtu.be/febgutDYP7w

About the Author

Annette Kämmerer is a psychologist and professor emerita at the Institute of Psychology at Heidelberg University in Germany. She sees patients in private practice and trains young psychotherapists.

Why the Secrets You Keep Are Hurting You

By Michael Slepian

It hurts to keep secrets. Secrecy is associated with lower well-being, worse health, and less satisfying relationships. Research has linked secrecy to increased anxiety, depression, symptoms of poor health, and even the more rapid progression of disease. There is a seemingly obvious explanation for these harms: Hiding secrets is hard work. You have to watch what you say. If asked about something related to the secret, you must be careful not to slip up. This could require evasion or even deception. Constant vigilance and concealment can be exhausting.

New research, however, suggests that the harm of secrets doesn't really come from the hiding after all. The real problem with keeping a secret is not that you have to hide it, but that you have to live with it, and think about it.

The concept of secrecy might evoke an image of two people in conversation, with one person actively concealing from the other. Yet, such concealment is actually uncommon. It is far more common to ruminate on our secrets. It is our tendency to mind-wander to our secrets that seems most harmful to well-being. Simply thinking about a secret can make us feel inauthentic. Having a secret return to mind, time and time again, can be tiring. When we think of a secret, it can make us feel isolated and alone.

To better understand the harms of secrecy, my colleagues and I first set out to understand what secrets people keep, and how often they keep them. We found that 97 percent of people have at least one secret at any given moment, and people have, on average, 13 secrets. A survey of more than 5,000 people found that common secrets include preferences, desires, issues surrounding relationships and sex, cheating, infidelity and violations of others' trust.

Across several studies, we asked participants to estimate how frequently they concealed their secret during conversations with others, and also how frequently they thought about the secret outside of social interactions. We found that the more frequently people simply thought about their secrets, the lower their well-being. The frequency of active concealment when interacting with others, however, had no relationship to well-being.

Following up this research, a new paper reveals why thinking about secrets is so harmful. Turning the question around, we examined the consequences of confiding secrets. We found that when a person confides a secret to a third party, it does not reduce how often they have to conceal the secret from others who are still kept in the dark. Rather, it reduces how often their mind wanders toward the secret in irrelevant moments.

The act of confiding a secret can feel cathartic and relieving. But mere catharsis is not enough. When confiding a secret, what is actually helpful is the conversation that follows. People report that when sharing a secret with another person, they often receive emotional support, useful guidance, and helpful advice. These forms of support make people feel more confident and capable in coping with the secret. When people find a healthier way of thinking about their secret, they ruminate less on it, and have improved well-being. Our studies suggest that what is important is talking to another person about a secret. A single conversation can lead to a healthier outlook and mind.

This new science of secrecy brings both good and bad news. The bad news is that even when we are not hiding our secrets, they are still very much with us, and can still hurt us. The good news is that even when we choose to still keep something secret, talking to another person can make the world of difference. Secrets don't have to hurt as much as they do.

About the Author

Michael Slepian is a professor of management at Columbia Business School. He studies the psychological effects of secrecy, the development and formation of trust, and deception detection. He maintains the KeepingSecrets.org project at Columbia University.

Section 3: Novel Medical and Drug Treatments for Anxiety and Depression

Novel Drug Therapies Could Tackle Treatment-Resistant Depression

By Husseini Manji, Joseph Hayes

Depression affects more than 264 million people of all ages globally. The World Health Organization ranks depression as one of the most debilitating diseases to society. It is the leading cause of disability worldwide and the psychiatric diagnosis most commonly associated with suicide, which accounts for nearly 800,000 deaths globally each year. Individuals suffering from depression may face an inability to manage life's demands and maintain social connections, affecting all aspects of their experiences, from school and employment to relationships and overall quality of life.

When it comes to treatment, approximately one third of those suffering from depression do not respond to two or more antidepressants and are considered treatment-resistant. Treatment-resistant depression is a chronic condition that places an increased emotional, functional and economic burden on the individual, their loved ones and society. It is also associated with greater morbidity, higher health care costs and various comorbid conditions.

While a number of antidepressants exist, they all work through changing the levels of brain-signaling molecules called monoaminergic neurotransmitters. New drug development for depression had stalled for a number of years, and many pharmaceutical companies have withdrawn from neuroscience entirely. But recent scientific advances have led to the development of novel antidepressants working via completely different mechanisms.

The brain is the most advanced, adaptive information processing system in existence–in large part because of its tremendous plasticity. Scientists have been building upon these neuroscience advances to develop completely novel, rapid-acting antidepressants. In this regard, considerable evidence has demonstrated that the regulation of two receptors–AMPA and NMDA–on many neurons that respond to the neurotransmitter glutamate control changes in the tiny junctions, or synapses, between neurons. Think of this synaptic plasticity as the mechanism by which the strength of information flow in these tiny gaps among brain cells is manipulated. Based on this research, scientists have demonstrated that blocking NMDA receptors on inhibitory neurons, thereby facilitating a burst of glutamate release, can exert rapid antidepressant effects in treatment-resistant depression. Indeed, this discovery led to the U.S. Food and Drug Administration and European Medicines Agency to approve esketamine, an NMDA antagonist for treatment-resistant depression, in 2019. (Esketamine is related chemically to ketamine, the anesthetic and psychedelic.) Agency approvals open up the possibility of developing the next generation of treatments in this class. Although at the very low doses used for treatment, esketamine is quite selective, it does target all NMDA receptors. It may be that some NMDA receptors are more responsible for its therapeutic antidepressant effects, whereas others may be more responsible for some side effects. Thus, the next generation of certain drugs that are NMDA antagonists *may* maintain efficacy while reducing some side effects.

Also in 2019 the FDA approved intravenous allopregnanolone as a first-in-class medication for the treatment of postpartum depression. Allopregnanolone is a neuroactive steroid, structurally similar to progesterone, that acts on GABA receptors and is believed to improve symptoms of depression and anxiety by amplifying GABAergic signaling throughout the brain. Zuranolone, an oral formulation of allopregnanolone, is currently being trialed more widely for treatment-resistant depression.

Psychedelics, such as psilocybin, also have a role to play. In a landmark exploratory trial published in the *New England Journal of Medicine* earlier this year, psilocybin was compared with the widely used antidepressant escitalopram. Although not powered to detect a difference between the drugs, a number of positive findings—levels of response and remission of symptoms—were more common in psilocybin-treated individuals. This has sparked renewed interest in psychedelic therapies as another avenue of drug discovery. Other novel approaches are also in the drug development pipeline, and each of them could add important new medications to treat this debilitating condition. The Orexin system regulates neuronal limbic circuits implicated in depression, and trials of Orexin 2 receptor antagonists are well underway. There is emerging evidence that neuroimmune factors may play a role, not only in neurodegenerative disorders but also in depression. Microglia are the resident immune cells in the brain, and efforts investigating P2x7 antagonists (which regulate microglial function) are underway. Finally scientists are exploring innovative ways to increase the levels of the body's own cannabinoids (rather than administering cannabis or other external sources of cannabinoids) as novel antidepressants.

Despite advances, unmet needs still exist in the mental health space, including ones related to tailoring specific treatments to specific patients, adequately treating the cognitive symptoms of schizophrenia, ensuring durable relapse prevention and persistence of efficacy for most conditions, and achieving better functional (not just symptomatic) outcomes.

It is these gaps in treatment that spur industry, academia and governments to continue research in depression with discovery and development of new and more effective treatments for people who still continue to experience symptoms and do not fully recover with existing treatments.

This is an opinion and analysis article, and the views expressed by the author or authors are not necessarily those of Scientific American.

About the Authors

Husseini Manji is a physician and global head of Science for Minds at Johnson & Johnson. Science for Minds is a new initiative bringing together the three pillars of science, innovation and society to catalyze the development of novel therapeutics for neuropsychiatric and neurodegenerative disease worldwide. He was previously the chief of the laboratory of pathophysiology and the director of the mood anxiety disorders program at the National Institutes of Health.

Joseph Hayes is currently a Wellcome Clinical Research Career Development fellow at the division of psychiatry at University College London, an honorary consultant in general adult psychiatry in Camden and Islington NHS Foundation Trust in England and an honorary public health consultant at Public Health England. He is on the editorial board of the British Journal of Psychiatry *and the* International Journal of Bipolar Disorders. *And he is a co-founder of juli Health.*

A Renaissance for Psychedelics Could Fill a Long-Standing Treatment Gap for Psychiatric Disorders

By Danielle Schlosser, Thomas R. Insel

Through a May 2021 article he wrote in the *Independent*, we learned about Steve Shorney, who lived with depression for most of his life despite years of psychotherapy, medication, yoga and many other attempts at holistic treatments. With his decision to enroll in a psilocybin clinical trial at Imperial College London, his life "radically changed." Psilocybin was different from every other treatment or experience he had had. As he recalled in the *Independent* article, "I had seen an alternative reality, another way of being, and knew beyond anything I'd known before that day that life is extraordinary. And in that moment I felt happier, more alive, and more Me than I imagined was possible."

The use of psychedelics, especially psilocybin and MDMA (also known as Ecstasy or Molly), is undergoing a renaissance. More than five decades ago psychedelics were an active area of research, with more than 40,000 patients receiving LSD or psilocybin for alcoholism, anxiety or depression. While we do not have rigorous clinical trials from that time, the use of these drugs garnered both scientific and public interest, with Hollywood celebrities such as Cary Grant promoting their use. But the War on Drugs, beginning during the Nixon years, led to a long, dark period where these drugs were lost to science, although they were still used in recreational and religious settings.

New studies have reignited the hope that psychedelics could be powerful medicines for mental disorders. In a *New England Journal of Medicine* report, two doses of the chemical from the psilocybin mushroom appeared as effective as six weeks of escitalopram (Lexapro), a standard antidepressant, for people with long-standing moderate-to-severe major depressive disorder (MDD). On many of the secondary measures of depression, such as remission of symptoms, psilocybin appeared better than the standard treatment, with 57 percent of subjects showing remission on psilocybin versus 28 percent in remission with escitalopram, although the authors caution that more research will be needed to confirm these results. In a study reported in *Nature Medicine*, MDMA was found to be more effective than placebo for people with severe post-traumatic stress disorder (PTSD). After three sessions with MDMA, 67 percent no longer met criteria for their diagnosis, and 33 percent showed complete remission, relative to 32 and 5 percent, respectively, after receiving a placebo.

Patients with disorders such as MDD and PTSD can certainly use more innovative, effective and safe treatments. Fewer than half of people with these disorders respond to medications or psychotherapy, and about a third of MDD patients have so-called treatment-refractory depression that fails to respond at all. Discovering new approaches to treat mental health conditions is critical. If psychedelics prove to be effective and safe for these disorders, they could be transformative in two interesting ways.

First, these medications appear to be effective after acute administration. Most psychiatric drugs, such as escitalopram for MDD, need to be taken for weeks, months or years to be effective. Presumably, they control symptoms but do not alter the disorder. When effective, psychedelics appear to confer long-term effects, sometimes after a single administration, suggesting that they are not simply symptom-reducing but disease-modifying. Moreover, some results from previous studies suggest that the benefits are long-lived, although the duration of effects in these recent studies remains to be determined.

Second, the studies thus far have focused on psychedelic-assisted psychotherapy—not just the drug but the experience in the context of structured, time-limited psychotherapy. We know that psychotherapy can be helpful for most mental disorders, yet therapy is rarely combined with medication. Psychedelics remind us of the potential for combining medication and therapy, a practice that is infrequent when most antidepressants and antianxiety drugs are prescribed by primary care physicians. This combination is especially promising, given that some evidence suggests that psychedelics enhance neuroplasticity, thereby opening up a "critical window" of time to develop a healthier mindset.

These new studies with psilocybin and MDMA focus on only two of the many psychedelic compounds with potential for medical use. Could this class of drugs, which includes LSD, mescaline and many lesser-known or yet to be discovered chemicals, revive drug development for psychiatry? Perhaps, but we need to be mindful that in a previous era, overexuberance about psychedelics led to a backlash with little scientific research and no translation to medical use.

It has been 50 years since psychedelics were classified as Schedule I compounds: drugs with "high potential for abuse and no currently accepted medical use." New science suggests that we may need to revisit this classification.

About the Authors

Danielle Schlosser is a psychologist and senior vice president of clinical innovation at Compass Pathways, which is conducting clinical trials of psilocybin. In her prior role, she was in charge of vision and strategy for the behavioral health portfolio at Verily Life Sciences, an Alphabet company, and she remains on the faculty at the University of California, San Francisco.

Thomas R. Insel is a psychiatrist and neuroscientist who served as director of the National Institute of Mental Health from 2002 to 2015. He is an adviser to Compass Pathways, as well as to several digital mental health companies, and author of Healing: Our Path from Mental Illness to Mental Health *(Penguin, 2022).*

Is an Antidepressant Right for You? Ask Your Brain Waves

By Karen Weintraub

People getting treated for depression often have to suffer through months of trial-and-error testing of different drugs to see which of them—if any—will help. For a long time, scientists and clinicians have hoped for a biological means of diagnosing depression or predicting which patients will do better on a given treatment. A new study takes a step toward the latter kind of prediction by finding a distinctive signature with the noninvasive technique of electroencephalography (EEG) to test who will benefit from one common antidepressant.

The study, published Monday in *Nature Biotechnology*, followed more than 300 people with depression as they began taking the drug sertraline (Zoloft) or a placebo. A computer algorithm could discern the EEGs of those who fared well on the drug from those who did not. Trained on one group, the algorithm also effectively predicted results in several others.

The work is preliminary and needs to be confirmed with further studies and expanded to include other treatments, such as different antidepressants, transcranial magnetic stimulation and psychotherapy. But "in my field, this, itself, is a huge step. We have not had the kind of predictors that are specific for a drug," says Madhukar Trivedi, a psychiatrist at the University of Texas Southwestern Medical Center's Peter O'Donnell Jr. Brain Institute, who oversaw the multisite trial.

Right now doctors give patients whichever antidepressant they like best, and then—for all choices in this class of drugs—they have to wait six to eight weeks to know whether it is working or not, says Amit Etkin, who also oversaw the research. If the drug does not work well, it might be another six weeks before they know whether a different dose or a new drug is more effective. Meanwhile many of the people who seek medication are at risk for suicide or too depressed to function normally.

"This very idea that we've accepted, as a field, as a world, that it takes eight weeks or more to see an antidepressant response, and that that's okay–that should never be okay," says Etkin, who is currently on leave from Stanford University to pursue commercialization of an EEG-based diagnostic. "We should be apologizing all the time about that, not accepting it." One in eight Americans currently takes an antidepressant, so improving the process of matching a patient to a medication could benefit a huge number of people, he says.

Tom Insel, former head of the National Institute of Mental Health and now an entrepreneur, thinks this approach–if proved through more research–could be extremely helpful for patients and doctors. "This is a real step forward. It's an important moment to say, 'Yes, we can indeed do better,'" says Insel, who was not involved in the new paper but was head of NIMH when it decided to fund the research. "If we could save these people a six-week trial on sertraline, that would save time and money and get better outcomes."

Today about 40 percent of patients will respond to the first drug they are given, Etkin says. In his study, about 65 percent of patients' whose EEG signature suggested they would respond well to sertraline did so. Even if the approach does not improve, as Etkin hopes it will, it is still substantially superior to the current method, he says.

Today's psychiatric drugs do not work better than a placebo for many people, which has given them the reputation of being ineffective. But the problem may be the diagnosis, not the drug, Etkin says. Maybe the current way we diagnose is imprecise, because it is not tied to the biology of the condition. "It's all subjective report," he says. If scientists could diagnose based on a biological marker, diagnoses would become more objective, and the same therapies would seem more effective because they would be better matched to patients who would benefit from them. An EEG has a lot of advantages as a diagnostic, Etkin says: it is relatively cheap, readily available and easy to administer.

The use of artificial intelligence is limited in a field such as mental health, where it is very challenging to get large data sets, he says. The researchers could not rely on the increasingly popular artificial intelligence technique known as deep learning, because it would require data from 100,000 patients or so to make predictions, which isn't feasible in psychiatry, he says. Instead Etkin and his colleagues created a simpler algorithm to mine the richness of EEG data and take advantage of the relatively large pool of patients they did have. Earlier efforts to find a signature without using AI failed, the paper shows, and patients' symptoms did not help to stratify them.

EEG measures electrical activity of the brain via electrodes placed on the skull. Some patterns of activity on the left side of the organ suggested that a patient would fare better on sertraline, Trivedi says. In the study, researchers used the same algorithm to try to find a signature–the absence of the same marker–that predicts which patients will respond well to transcranial magnetic stimulation (TMS), which delivers repeated magnetic pulses to areas of the brain thought to be involved in depression.

"From a patient perspective, that is a very valuable step," says Martijn Arns, another author of the paper and research director of the Brainclinics Foundation in the Netherlands. "Rather than using 'stepped care,' where a patient is started on the 'simplest' treatment and escalated every time [that person] does not respond, we can now guide someone more quickly to the right treatment that will work for [him or her] using a biomarker."

Sebastian Olbrich, an EEG researcher who was not involved in the new study, says that although he considers the paper a "great piece of work," he is concerned that the researchers team did not train their algorithm on TMS before drawing their conclusions. "They only trained it on one treatment option and then applied it to another," which isn't appropriate, he says.

Still, Olbrich, a psychiatrist and president of the International Pharmaco EEG Society, says he is eager to see the study expanded to other depression treatments. "If you have this for several treatment options, this is a really great step for psychiatry," he says.

Trivedi says he would ultimately like to develop an EEG test that could identify the signature of depression before a person suffered its symptoms. He adds that he has begun a study with about 1,200 volunteers whom he plans to follow over time. He will check in with them a few times a year to begin to develop predictive models about who will experience depression and who will recover from it.

About the Author

Karen Weintraub is a staff writer at USA Today, *where she covers COVID, vaccine development and other health issues.*

Fighting Depression with Magnets

By Kasra Zarei

Depression and antidepressant use are at all-time highs in the year 2017, but for about a third of those affected, depression still doesn't get better with medication—and for these patients, transcranial magnetic stimulation (TMS), which uses powerful magnets to stimulate brain cells noninvasively, can be a viable option.

To be clear, TMS isn't new; it was first approved by the FDA in 2008. What's new is that the evidence for its safety and effectiveness has only gotten stronger. TMS is now generally covered by insurance companies for treatment-resistant depression, and new studies have shown that combining it with traditional treatments like psychotherapy can lead to significantly higher response rates. Some scientists also now believe TMS can be a dominant therapy compared to antidepressants, based on its lower cost, higher net monetary benefit and better quality of life outcomes produced. Although there are still many questions about TMS left unanswered, it is a treatment with a strong presence in fighting depression and much promise as *personalized* TMS grows closer to becoming a reality.

When Medication Fails: Treatment-Resistant Depression

According to the World Health Organization, an estimated 350 million people worldwide suffer from depression, making it the leading cause of disability worldwide. As many as 30 percent of people with depression are resistant to medication, and show suicide thoughts and attempts, and an overall poor quality of life. With traditional treatment options ineffective, these patients need a solution.

One such person is 63-year-old Brenda Griffith, a retired nurse, mother and grandmother.

"My depression started prior to my late 30s when my life wasn't great. I couldn't think clearly a lot of the time and it was difficult working as a nurse. I couldn't enjoy life at all," Griffith says.

Griffith was diagnosed with depression in the early 1990s by her psychiatrist, James Beeghly, and was subsequently prescribed nearly every antidepressant medication.

Antidepressants are the most commonly used treatment for depression. New data from the CDC reports that an estimated one in eight Americans over the age of 12 have taken antidepressants. Most patients with depression report some improvement in response to medication, but for Griffith, the antidepressants just made things worse.

"My depression progressively got worse as I took the medications. I took over 12 medications over years, and nothing seemed to work," Griffith said. "What's worse is I also experienced terrible side effects like nausea all the time."

It turns out, Griffith had treatment-resistant depression, a term used to refer to cases of depression where the patient still exhibits symptoms of depression following two or more antidepressant treatments.

As another treatment option, Griffith started electroconvulsive therapy (ECT), an invasive therapy used for more severe cases of depression that passes electric currents through the brain. ECT is used to treat severe cases of treatment-resistant depression but carries risks and side effects including memory loss, confusion, and physical effects–all of which were experienced by Griffith.

"ECT saved my life, but it wasn't enough for me to function normally. I had to give up nursing," Griffith said. "I was on ECT for 15 years but because of my long-term ECT, learning new things was difficult. I was so afraid of the memory loss getting worse, I didn't want to do it anymore."

With both antidepressants and ECT unable to improve Griffith's life, she began her last option: TMS, which had been approved by the FDA for treatment-resistant depression.

The TMS Experience for Depression

With transcranial magnetic stimulation, a small electromagnetic coil is placed against a patient's head at a precise location. For patients with depression, this location is the left frontal cortex of the brain that has historically been shown to be less active in people with depression.

TMS attempts to fix the lack of activity in the left frontal cortex through providing daily stimulations that rewire and cause the cortex to become more excitable and produce a long-lasting antidepressant effect.

The noninvasive nature of TMS is what makes it appealing compared to ECT. When TMS was first clinically used, there was some hesitation in its widespread adoption due to concerns about its safety, mainly whether it would accidentally cause seizures. However, recent studies show that there are no major safety concerns with TMS.

"The term noninvasive refers to the fact that no surgery is required," said Aaron Boes, a TMS expert at the University of Iowa. "In fact, the safety data for TMS is very strong–there are no major cognitive side-effects in patients and the risk of seizures is less than 0.1 percent."

The standard TMS treatment happens in 40-minute sessions each day of the week for 4–6 weeks. Each individual treatment session can cost $300–$500 and there are typically 30 to 40 sessions in a course of TMS therapy. Insurance coverage for TMS used to be spotty, but now, the majority of insurance companies and federal programs cover TMS therapy for treatment-resistant depression.

During a standard TMS session, a patient can read or talk with other people. Furthermore, the patient can drive to and from the TMS sessions, so they don't need someone to constantly supervise them.

"The whole treatment setup was fantastic–the coil that provides the stimulation feels like a gentle woodpecker on your head. I wasn't nervous about it at all, I was comfortable," Griffith says. "It's a mild discomfort when you first start but you get used to it and the side effects are so limited. It can be noisy, but you wear earplugs."

Three weeks into her TMS treatment, Griffith's condition started improving. People around Griffith, including her psychiatrist, noticed the differences in her since the treatment.

"TMS made Brenda better and more like her natural self," Beeghly says. "When I first started seeing her as my patient many years ago, I saw a picture of her smiling. I didn't see that kind of smile from her for decades. I saw it with TMS. It's been liberating for her. She has more control over her life in many ways. Instead of sleeping, she now spends time with her family."

On average, patients tend to respond to TMS after two to four weeks, and the response rates are encouraging.

"For patients who have tried and failed at least two antidepressants in the current episode, the data is the rule of thirds," says Mark George, a pioneer in using TMS for depression who leads the Brain Stimulation Laboratory at the Medical University of South Carolina. "About one third will get remission with no symptoms left, another one third will get response with their symptoms cut in half, and unfortunately one third will get no response."

About 58 percent of TMS-treated patients will have a positive response, defined as a reduction in their depression by 50 percent of more, and 37 percent of all patients will have complete remission of depression.

A recent cost-effectiveness analysis study conducted by scientists identified TMS as the dominant therapy compared to antidepressant medication given the current costs of both. In the study, scientists used simulation modeling to determine that TMS can be provided at a lower cost, and a higher net monetary benefit with better quality of life outcomes compared to antidepressant medication. Despite these statistics, there is a lot of treatment variability with TMS.

"TMS can produce a durable treatment response, but it is not a cure. It tends to last around nine months, with variability, with continued treatment often needed," Boes says.

What We Still Don't Know

Maintaining and extending the TMS treatment response is an active area of research. TMS experts believe this can be accomplished with individualized treatment protocols.

"Like many areas of medicine, TMS is a treatment that might someday be customized so it is delivered in a way that is personalized to match the individual patient's brain abnormality," says Linda Carpenter, a TMS expert and professor of psychiatry at Brown University.

Carpenter also adds that before personalized TMS services become a reality, scientists still need to discover how to make the clinical improvement from TMS last longer before a depressive relapse occurs. Most scientists studying TMS believe that greater consistency in treatment responses and longer-lasting effects could be achieved if they were able to identify more precise and personalized stimulation targets in patients' brains.

"Many people think that better science behind the targeting, precisely where the TMS 'coil' is placed on the scalp, could bring about better antidepressant results," Carpenter says. "There is also interest in learning about other activities such as psychotherapy, brain training, or exercise that might be synergistically paired with TMS therapy to get the maximal therapeutic effect."

In fact, scientists just recently published a study that combined TMS and psychotherapy to treat patients with depression. What is exciting is that they observed response and remission rates significantly higher than those predicted by the "rule of thirds."

There are even more questions about TMS that, if answered, could improve treatment. For instance, scientists still do not exactly know what frequency and intensity is needed for the stimulation, how many sessions should be administered and how the treatment works to bring about the resolution of depression symptoms.

"We still do not fully understand the exact translational cascade that TMS starts that ends up fixing depression," George says.

Despite these unanswered questions, the evidence supporting the clinical use of TMS for treatment-resistant depression is still strong. A recent study of treatment in 42 U.S.-based clinical TMS sites that treated 307 patients with major depressive disorder confirmed that TMS is an effective treatment for people unable to benefit from antidepressants. TMS is increasingly viable and, according to Carpenter, some scientists believe there could potentially be a future generation of similar brain stimulation devices that are safe for administration at home.

Although TMS is not a miracle cure and other treatments should be tried first, it is more viable and validated today than ever before, and provides an option for people like Griffith with treatment-resistant depression. Griffith hopes her experience can be educational for other individuals and their families in similar situations.

"Depression affects your life, and it affects your family," Griffith says. "But you have to be open to changes. You have to fight depression and know that there are options."

The views expressed are those of the author(s) and are not necessarily those of Scientific American.

About the Author

Kasra is a freelance writer covering science, health and the environment. He was a 2020 AAAS Mass Media Fellow.

Experimental Brain Implant Could Personalize Depression Therapy

By Gary Stix

Sarah remembers what it was like both before and after the treatment. The 36-year old vividly recalls how, after her depression lifted, she had to readapt to performing the tasks other people do routinely each day. Even the simple act of looking at a menu took readjustment.

"I also had to learn, relearn," she said at a press briefing, "how to actually have opinions about things and actually pick something on a menu and order it and not just go along with what everyone else wanted. Because I was so used to the fact that I couldn't make decisions, that [ability], over the last five years...., just atrophied and disappeared."

Sarah's intractable depression, which had not responded even to electroconvulsive therapy, yielded after an experimental treatment conducted at the University of California, San Francisco. The treatment detects depression-related brain activity and then applies electrical stimulation at a targeted location to relieve symptoms. The device used for the procedure has already been approved for treating epilepsy by providing brain stimulation after it registers electrical patterns that predict an oncoming seizure.

In the October 4 study in *Nature Medicine*, the researchers describe how they set about to find a stimulation site using electrodes to probe emotion circuitry in Sarah's brain. As they looked, they found that one site might lower anxiety and that another might increase energy levels.

When the team activated a site deep in Sarah's brain in a reward-related area called the ventral striatum, she had an immediate reaction. Sarah was doing needlework during one session to distract herself from negative thoughts when a stimulus was applied to that spot. Her mood changed quickly. In a U.C.S.F. article about the treatment, she recounted her surprise at feeling that she was enjoying what she was doing–experiencing, in fact, a sense of "glee and happiness."

The researchers also wanted to know when to provide a stimulus. Previous research on activating neural circuits to relieve depression using other deep-brain stimulation (DBS) techniques have met with mixed results. Earlier attempts did not map the brain to take into account the fact that depression may vary among individuals.

These efforts also applied continuous stimulation. The U.C.S.F. researchers suspect that the effectiveness of this type of treatment depends on knowing when an electrode should be activated in anticipation of symptoms growing more severe, similar to the approach taken with epilepsy.

They looked for what they call a "biomarker" that could supply such an alert. They found it in the amygdala, which mediates emotional processes and is also connected to the striatum. High-frequency neural activity–"gamma oscillations"–in the amygdala indicated when symptoms were about to get worse.

Last year the team implanted the about $30,000 epilepsy device, Neuropace RNS, in the right hemisphere of Sarah's brain. An electrical wire goes to the amygdala to detect gamma activity. When present, a warning flashes back to a thin metal disk placed in the skull. The disk, a neurostimulator, then transmits a signal along a separate wire to the striatum to tamp down feelings of sadness and depression.

Stimulation is applied in a short six-second burst and then turns off until another gamma warning is received. This intermittent switching on adds up to no more than 30 minutes a day. But for Sarah, it has made a difference. "The device has kept my depression at bay," Sarah said at the press briefing, "allowing me to return to my best self and rebuild a life worth living."

When tried with new patients, the therapy will again be personalized. Others will also undergo the process of electrical probing to look for brain stimulation areas most suited to their depression. But the challenges accompanying Sarah's case make the

U.C.S.F. researchers optimistic. "We didn't know if we were going to be able to treat her depression at all because it was so severe," said Katherine Scangos, a U.C.S.F. physician and lead author of the *Nature Medicine* paper, at the press briefing.

Longtime DBS researchers also took notice. "This is an interesting and important proof of principle case," says Helen Mayberg, a neurologist at the Icahn School of medicine at Mount Sinai, who has been a pioneer in earlier DBS studies for depression and was not involved in the new study. "Time will tell if this approach substantively improves on simpler open-loop strategies [without biomarkers]."

Andres Lozano, a professor of neurosurgery at the University of Toronto and a collaborator of Mayberg's, who was also not involved in the *Nature Medicine* paper, says that the work is an "exciting finding that leads to a more personalized and 'just in time' approach to delivering brain stimulation in depression when and where it is needed." He adds that "several questions remain, including the generalizability of these biomarkers across patients and whether the application of stimulation produces more than merely acute changes but indeed an enduring benefit."

Sarah is just one patient. The study she enrolled in was a "proof of concept"–what researchers call an "*n* of one." "We're still learning; we're at the very, very beginning of trying to understand how this works," says U.C.S.F. neurosurgeon Edward Chang, who is co-senior author of the study. U.C.S.F. is in the process of lining up 11 additional patients. The new research could ultimately provide a better idea of whether targeting just the right brain circuit can lift the penumbra that hangs over a severely depressed person.

About the Author

Gary Stix is a senior editor at Scientific American.

Can a Pill That Boosts "Resilience" Treat Depression?

By Gary Stix

Self-help books often extoll the value of resilience. Last year one such primer–*Bounce: Overcoming Adversity, Building Resilience and Finding Joy*–proclaimed: "By strengthening your inner power, your ability to handle stressful situations and your skill in persevering after setbacks threaten to fell you, you'll develop real resilience–you'll develop grit."

This implies weathering adverse life events is a character trait to be cultivated. Exercising, eating right and giving yourself mental pep talks certainly may help. But neuroscientists are learning the story is not quite so simple, and that some people are likely better equipped from birth to deal with adversity. During the last 15 years discoveries about why some brains excel at resisting stress have initiated a search for new drugs to treat depression and post-traumatic stress disorder by enhancing psychological resilience. One of these compounds has now entered early-stage clinical trials.

If the drug is safe and works, it will undoubtedly encounter strong demand; depression–the world's leading cause of mental disability–never enters full remission in more than half the patients treated with psychotherapies and existing antidepressants.

But depression does not affect everyone, and the molecular biology of resilience for psychiatric disorders can be clearly seen by inspecting the brains of lab animals. About a third of mice exposed to severe stress (in the form of aggressive attacks by other rodents) seem to breeze through these assaults without developing the social withdrawal, listlessness or other depression and traumalike symptoms displayed by most of their rodent lab-mates.

Observing this seemingly adaptive behavior, investigators started to probe the genetics and neurochemistry that distinguish the more resistant animals. In stressed mice there is a dramatic rise in the activity of certain genes in the nervous system—as if these rodents' brains had set in motion a set of protective measures to cope with the trauma. "Manyfold more genes were regulated in the resilient animals than in the susceptible animals across several brain regions," says Eric Nestler, director of The Friedman Brain Institute at Icahn School of Medicine at Mount Sinai. "That was a real surprise to us." (Nestler was at The University of Texas Southwestern Medical Center when his group started studying what researchers call chronic social defeat stress.)

New York City's Mount Sinai Hospital has become a nexus for resilience research, with studies conducted by several laboratories on both the psychology and neurobiology of adapting to stress. In 2014 pharmacologist and neuroscientist Ming-Hu Han and a group of his Mount Sinai colleagues published a paper in *Science* showing how out-of-whack electrical signaling in neurons populating the brain's reward system could explain why some lab animals were susceptible to depression whereas others remained resilient.

Looking inside the brains of animals exposed to chronic social defeat stress, the scientists observed hyperactive firing of neurons in the ventral tegmental area (VTA), a critical part of a reward circuit. When things go awry, this manic firing of cells in the VTA contributes to the lack of motivation experienced in depression.

The resilient mice, however, held a surprise for Han and his team. The VTAs in their brains exhibited even greater levels of frenzied electrical activity than those of their more vulnerable counterparts—but only for a brief period. In the naturally resilient animals the higher neural activity seemed to induce a counterreaction that resulted in the subsequent quieting of overactive neurons. "This is one of the most important unexpected findings in the 2014 *Science* paper," Han says. "Too big a pathophysiological alteration triggers a compensatory rebound."

The Han team took things one step further to see if they could help the nonresilient animals through artificial means. When the researchers gave the mice a drug called lamotrigine, often prescribed for bipolar disorder, the animals' brain activity mimicked that of their resilient counterparts: The neurons in the already hyperactive VTA started firing even more intensely, followed by a lull and abatement of depression symptoms.

Around this time the various resilience research groups at Mount Sinai convened for a monthly gathering referred to informally as "The Depression Club." Han told the group about a set of compounds—all existing drugs—that help open channels in the outer membrane of cells in the VTA. When dosed with the drugs, these neurons, which produce the signaling molecule dopamine, let positively charged ions leave the cell, thereby damping the cells' hyperactive firing. This in turn tamps down depression symptoms. Based on Han's presentation to the Depression Club, the group decided to move forward with a clinical trial in patients. The study—led by James Murrough, assistant professor of psychiatry and director of the Mood and Anxiety Disorders Program at Mount Sinai—chose the epilepsy drug ezogabine, which was given to 18 patients in a pilot trial.

Brain scans showed the drug affected the same reward circuit that it did in animals. "It was successful in the sense that we did see antidepressant effects, with the important caveat that there was no placebo group," Murrough says. A larger placebo-controlled clinical trial, sponsored by the National Institute of Mental Health (NIMH), is now underway. (GlaxoSmithKline has decided to stop marketing ezogabine but other existing drugs that also operate by tweaking potassium channels in brain cells—or a wholly new class of compounds—could serve in its place.)

The idea of a resilience pill seems compelling to some researchers not directly involved with the Mount Sinai research. "The ability to provide a treatment that can increase stress resiliency at the cellular level, and hopefully also the behavioral level, would be a much welcomed addition to our antidepressant armamentarium," says Gerard Sanacora, a professor of psychiatry at Yale University School of Medicine and director of the Yale Depression Research Program. He cautions, however, about drawing too many conclusions from animal studies and early-stage clinical trials. He cites his own group's experience with a novel antidepressant candidate that initially looked promising but failed in a placebo-controlled trial.

Moving forward with a potential resilience pill is warranted, however, notes Robert Sapolsky, a Stanford University professor of neuroscience. "There's such a massive number of people with serious depression who aren't helped by current drugs that it's most definitely worth a try." The approach pursued by Mount Sinai investigators "has been really novel," Sapolsky says, "focusing on very reductive mechanisms explaining why VTA neurons become hyperactive in mice destined for stress-induced depression, and not in resistant animals."

One caveat comes from David Nutt of Imperial College London. He points out that like new resilience drug candidates, standard depression treatments like Prozac diminish hyperactivity in neurons—but in a different set of cells. "I think that resilience is how the current antidepressant drugs work," Nutt says. The neuropsychopharmacologist suggests a more novel approach might involve psychedelic drugs such as psilocybin, which have potential antidepressant effects.

Ezogabine represents only one means to potentially enhance resilience. Researchers at Mount Sinai and elsewhere are considering other ways of regulating the reward system as well as modulating gene activity and the brain's signaling molecules, or neurotransmitters.

Unlike many clinical trials that emphasize relief of symptoms as their primary objective, the ezogabine study's goal is to gauge how well the therapy addresses some of the biological underpinnings of depression—in this case, whether the drug lessens the hyperactivity of the reward circuit that includes VTA neurons. The NIMH has focused recently on targeting disease mechanisms in research it funds, because symptoms overlap for many psychiatric disorders. Whether this approach works better in developing drugs for psychiatric disorders remains to be proved. But it is worth exploring; conventional clinical trials have repeatedly come up empty.

About the Author

Gary Stix is a senior editor at Scientific American.

Why I Get My Brain Zapped

By David Levine

Almost seven percent of U.S. adults–about 15.7 million people–are diagnosed with major depression disorder, according to the National Institute of Mental Health (NIMH). The Centers for Disease Control and Prevention report that depression causes 200 million lost workdays each year at a cost to employers of between $17 billion and $44 billion. The statistics for anxiety disorders are not great either. The most common mental illnesses in the U.S., they affect 40 million adults age 18 and older, costing the economy more than $42 billion a year.

In my twenties, I developed panic disorder. I failed to get better on most medications and therapy. As I reported in an article earlier this year, it took me years to find a medication that worked. Because it took me so long to be diagnosed and treated properly, I have always been interested in alternative treatments for depression and anxiety.

Two years ago I attended two sessions at the World Science Festival on the use of electrical therapy to treat depression and anxiety. The first event was Spark of Genius? Awakening a Better Brain, a panel discussion moderated by ABC News Chief Health & Medical Editor Richard Besser. The panel discussed what is known about treating the brain and the ethical and legal complications of brain enhancement. (You can watch it online at the World Science Festival website.)

The second panel, "Electric Medicine and the Brain" was moderated by John Rennie, former editor in chief of *Scientific American.* His panel focused on the use of "electroceuticals," a term coined by researchers at GlaxoSmithKline to refer to all implantable devices being used to treat mental illnesses and being explored in the treatment of metabolic, cardiovascular and inflammatory disorders.

I am excited about the potential of these treatments because the existing treatments such as Prozac, Zoloft and Lexapro don't work for everyone. They didn't work for me. Talk therapies, especially cognitive behavioral therapy can also be effective, but they are expensive and insurance companies place limits on the number of sessions available to patients. Because of this, and the desire for a quick fix, most people with depression and/or anxiety opt for drugs.

But there are drawbacks to medication. First, it can take up to six weeks for antidepressants to work fully (they treat both depression and anxiety disorders). They have side effects such as weight gain, sedation and sexual problems. Antidepressant medications are contraindicated in pregnant women. The U.S. Food and Drug Administration (FDA) has ruled they should not be used for children and young adults up to age 25 as they increase the risk of suicidal ideation. And they don't always work either. A study in the *Journal of the American Medical Association* found that compared with placebo, antidepressant medications benefited people with severe depression but that the effects were "minimal or nonexistent, on average, in patients with mild or moderate symptoms."

Given the limitations of treatments for anxiety and depression, I was surprised to read the mostly negative view of electrical treatments by John Horgan in these pages. In his article, he writes "rather than developing ever-more-potent therapies, psychiatrists and others in the mental-health industry seem merely to recycle old ones." While it's true that electrical cures are not new, there is good evidence that they are useful and should have a place in the treatment of mental disorders.

As Horgan pointed out electroconvulsive therapy (ECT) has the best track record. It is highly effective. But for those who have seen *One Flew Over the Cuckoo's Nest* it's not an ideal treatment.

Transcranial magnetic stimulation (TMS)–which noninvasively administers brief, magnetic pulses to the brain–is a less "shocking" approach than ECT, and is being used at major medical centers. The treatment, which must be done under medical supervision, consists of passing high currents through an electromagnetic coil adjacent to a patient's scalp. The targeted magnetic pulses stimulate the circuits in the brain that are underactive in patients with depression, with the goal of restoring normal function and mood. The FDA has cleared TMS for the treatment of major depressive disorder in adults for whom medication did not work. For most patients, treatment is administered daily for four to six weeks, 40 minutes a session. Studies, including one by the National Institute of Mental Health (NIMH) have demonstrated its efficacy and safety in treating major depression.

For those interested, the NIMH has an excellent review article of other brain stimulation therapies including Deep Brain Stimulation and Vagus Nerve Stimulation as well as more information on TMS.

I have been using the Fisher Wallace Stimulator, a portable, battery-powered generator permitted by the FDA for symptomatic relief of insomnia, anxiety and depression, and for treating chronic pain (although the agency recently proposed imposing new restrictions on such devices). It is a cranial electrotherapy stimulation (CES) device which stimulates the brain to produce serotonin and other neurochemicals. It is designed to be used for 20 minutes twice a day and may be used with or without medication in consultation with your doctor.

For me, the best part is that unlike ECT, TMS or other therapies, the Fisher Wallace Stimulator can be used at home and there is no risk of seizures. Your doctor has to prescribe it and you can buy the device on the company website for $699 (there is a $100 discount for Medicare, Medicaid, Veteran and First Responder Families) but can return it for a full discount if it doesn't work within 30 days. Some insurance plans will pay for the device when it is prescribed for chronic pain. Mine did.

The Fisher Wallace Stimulator has been shown effective in many studies including one in the *Journal of Affective Disorders*. The results of a pilot study for the treatment of bipolar disorder was published last year.

I have been using the Fisher Wallace Stimulator for about six years to help with my anxiety and chronic pain. I occasionally use it for insomnia as well. When I travel to a different time zone, I find it helpful with jet lag, although it is not one of the conditions it was set out to treat. I find it relaxing. I don't feel like I am "shocking my brain," and it reminds me of how I felt when I practiced transcendental meditation in college.

I agree with Horgan that we need better treatments for depression and anxiety. But I think that although much remains unknown, electrical stimulation of the brain is a good alternative for many people, especially those who have failed to respond to traditional therapies.

The views expressed are those of the author(s) and are not necessarily those of Scientific American.

SSRIs May Help Us See the Glass Half Full

By Roni Jacobson

Prozac, Paxil, Celexa, Zoloft, Lexapro. These so-called selective serotonin reuptake inhibitors (SSRIs) are among the most widely prescribed drugs in the U.S. Although they are typically used to treat depression and anxiety disorders, they are also prescribed off-label for conditions such as chronic pain, premature ejaculation, bulimia, irritable bowel syndrome, premenstrual syndrome and hot flashes.

Even if you have never taken an SSRI, chances are you know someone who has. About one in every 10 American adults is being prescribed one now. For women aged 40 to 59 years old, the proportion increases to one in four.

Raising Serotonin

SSRIs block the body from reabsorbing serotonin, a neurotransmitter mostly found in the brain, spinal cord and digestive tract whose roles include regulation of mood, appetite, sexual function and sleep. Specifically, SSRIs bind to the protein that carries serotonin between nerve cells—called SERT, for serotonin transporter—intercepting it before it can escort the released neurotransmitter back into the cell. This action leaves more active serotonin in the body, a chemical effect that is supposed to spur feelings of happiness and well-being.

But there are hints that SSRIs are doing something other than simply boosting serotonin levels. First, people vary in their response to SSRIs: Studies have shown that the drugs are not very effective for mild to moderate depression, but work well when the disorder is severe. If low serotonin were the only culprit in depression, SSRIs would be more uniformly helpful in alleviating symptoms. Second, it takes weeks after starting an SSRI for depression and anxiety to lift even though changes in serotonin ought to happen pretty much right away.

Changing Emotional Bias

Some data suggest that SSRIs may also lessen negativity by calming the amygdala, a brain region that governs fear, among other emotions. People with depression and anxiety typically pay excessive attention to unpleasant social and environmental cues, which creates a "negative emotional bias" in the way they interpret their experiences, says psychopharmacologist Phil Cowen of the University of Oxford. In their brain, the amygdala is overactive whereas the prefrontal cortex, which keeps emotions in check, is unusually quiet. Neuroimaging studies indicate that SSRIs lessen these negative biases by inhibiting the amygdala and improving communication between the prefrontal cortex and the emotional processing areas, Cowen says.

Learning

SSRIs have also been found to stimulate nerve growth in the hippocampus, a brain structure involved in learning and memory. Imaging studies have indicated that people with depression may have fewer connections among neurons; so one theory suggests that SSRIs alleviate depression by encouraging neural growth and plasticity. Cowen hypothesizes that the new connections form as people with depression relearn old emotional associations in a way that puts their experiences in a more positive light. This learning might be necessary for recovery–and the time it takes to gain a new perspective might partly explain why SSRIs take so long to work.

Appetites

SSRIs have various effects on other parts of the body, too. Sexual dysfunction, for example, may occur because the drugs limit tension in blood vessels, making it difficult to achieve genital arousal. One person's side effect may be another's salve, however: men suffering from premature ejaculation are sometimes prescribed SSRIs. SSRIs also alter appetite signaling, accounting for two other common side effects, nausea and weight gain. Relatedly, serotonin levels in the gut can trigger intestinal contractions and secretions, potentially explaining why SSRIs help ameliorate irritable bowel syndrome and other digestive disorders.

About the Author

Roni Jacobson is a science journalist based in New York City who writes about psychology and mental health.

Section 4: New Therapies and Lifestyle Changes for Anxiety and Depression

Adolescent Mental Health? There's a 'Vaccine' for That

By Tamar Mendelson and Laura Clary

Ask any teenager if they would like to talk about mindfulness and mood thermometers with their peers a dozen times in one school year, and most would decline the opportunity. But ask them instead if they would like a vaccine to ward off the worst mental health impacts of the past year and a half, and most would raise their hands without thinking.

Adolescence is a critical time for mental health, and most teens have an intimate relationship with stress. Before the pandemic, one out of every five U.S. teens developed a mental disorder, with half of all mental disorders occurring by age 14 and three quarters by the mid-20s. During the pandemic, approximately 40,000 children lost a parent, and many young people have been exposed to other traumas, such as food insecurity and homelessness, that increase risk for depression, anxiety and post-traumatic stress disorder. The pandemic will likely cause a spike in youth mental health problems, with long-term psychological fallout.

The good news is that, for youth, schools are an effective setting for preventing mental health problems. School-based interventions that enhance students' capacity to regulate their emotions in healthy ways, such as reframing a problem positively, have proven effective at preventing or reducing mental health problems.

Our research offers one example: our team delivered a 12-session group prevention program called RAP (Relax, be Aware and do a Personal rating) Club to eighth graders in 29 Baltimore City public schools. Most schools served marginalized communities where poverty limits family prospects and youth are exposed to high rates of violence and other trauma.

RAP Club included mindfulness practices, such as breathing breaks with a "mood thermometer," to teach students nonjudgmental awareness of feelings and thoughts. Role-playing gave youth tools to promote positive communications. To demonstrate how pent-up stress affects the body, students shook up a bottle of seltzer until the liquid exploded; that was always a favorite.

Four months later, assessments with RAP Club students showed they had significantly fewer trauma symptoms than students who did not participate. And group discussions with RAP Club students highlighted other benefits. They talked about improved coping. "I been dealing with stress way better.... Way, way better," said one boy.

Other students agreed. "When I get distressed... I used to smoke to get it off my mind. See now... I don't do it as much." "When I'm angry–I don't just snap on everybody."

Students saw changes in their sense of self. "I really used to have negative thoughts about myself, about the world.... Now I'm way more confident."

And they described improved mental health: "Depression went away from me...I used to stay in my room a lot, listen to sad, depressing music, and just not talk to nobody. RAP Club... helped me–I dance more. I talk to my mother about everything now ... we all happy and all that. Our life just changed."

COVID then provided an unexpected opportunity for a natural experiment. We contacted and assessed a subset of approximately 150 trial participants during the pandemic, one to four years after they completed our programming. Youth who did not take part in RAP Club showed increased anxiety during the pandemic, which makes sense. We are in extraordinarily stressful times.

However, youth who participated in RAP Club, who learned how to manage the stress generated from the prepandemic hardships they faced, did not show a significant increase in anxiety. The program had provided a degree of immunization against this new batch of stress.

When this program began, we did not anticipate COVID-19 and the many ways it has disrupted childhood. As we dig deeper though, we start to see the potential of mental health interventions to protect against negative impacts of future trauma exposure.

As a new academic year approaches, most policy makers and educators will look to "check the box" and provide some sort of programming, or teacher training, that acknowledges the emotional damage the pandemic has inflicted. But these new findings show urgency for programming that goes much further.

Schools need resources to deliver evidence-based programs in an ongoing fashion to promote and protect student mental health. These programs need to be culturally and developmentally appropriate and delivered in a coordinated fashion across grades K-12. While all students should receive universal group programming, more intensive services should be offered to those needing additional support. Finally, program evaluation is critical to assess whether programs are effective and for whom they work best. Partnerships with universities can support data collection and analyses. Students' and parents' perspectives on what works must also shape solutions.

In coordination with student vaccination efforts, school leaders and policy makers should leverage the potential for school mental health programs to serve as "mental health vaccines." As one of our focus group participants noted, "When you learn your feelings, you kind of find like inner peace. That happens, yeah." We owe it to our nation's youth to provide all the emotional protection we have available.

This is an opinion and analysis article; the views expressed by the author or authors are not necessarily those of Scientific American.

About the Authors

Tamar Mendelson, Ph.D., and Laura Clary, Ph.D., are faculty members in the Department of Mental Health at the Johns Hopkins Bloomberg School for Public Health. Dr. Mendelson is a Bloomberg Professor of American Health and directs the Johns Hopkins Center for Adolescent Health.

Can Talk Therapy Help People Who Are Unable to Experience Joy?

By Dina Fine Maron

Imagine living a life without the ability to relish the delectable sweetness of ice cream, the joy of getting together with an old friend or a small triumph at work. People who suffer from a condition called anhedonia find it hard to enjoy much of anything. They are not necessarily sad, but feel very little pleasure in daily existence—or none at all. Finding the motivation to socialize, take action in the world and access life's rewards is painfully elusive for them.

Anhedonia is a common symptom of depression and one of the so-called "negative symptoms" of schizophrenia (as opposed to "positive" ones such as delusions), but it is not present in all patients with these illnesses. It also afflicts some people with bipolar disorder, substance abuse and Parkinson's disease as well as an unknown number of individuals with no other diagnosed brain disorder.

The biology of anhedonia is not well understood, although it has been linked to abnormal volume in brain structures related to seeking rewards and, according to brain scans, less activity in these areas. Anhedonia is also associated with a poor prognosis, including heightened risk of suicidal thoughts.

The condition is difficult to treat successfully. Drugs commonly used for depression such as selective serotonin reuptake inhibitors (SSRIs) can help relieve hopelessness and other negative feelings but they do not necessarily promote positive feelings or joy.

Fortunately for sufferers, dozens of studies looking at anhedonia are currently underway or have recently been completed. Several involve drug treatments, ranging from a dietary supplement to a form of amphetamine to experimental medications. In addition, some clinicians report preliminary evidence showing the anesthetic ketamine might be useful in treating anhedonia.

Psychiatry professors Moria Smoski of Duke University Medical Center and Gabriel Dichter of the University of North Carolina at Chapel Hill School of Medicine are co-leading one of the first clinical trials targeting this condition with customized talk therapy. They have begun recruiting 210 patients to be part of a five-year randomized trial. Half will receive an experimental therapy that is a tweaked version of a common treatment for depression called behavioral activation therapy, which involves giving patients very concrete tasks and goals that reflect the patients' values. The other half will be placed in a control group that will learn mindfulness techniques.

Patients getting the experimental therapy might, for example, be told to attend a certain number of parties or gatherings each week, even if that seems unappealing. Or they might have a goal of making dinner for a friend who just got out of the hospital. The theory behind this approach, the researchers say, is that if you take part in such activities and find they were somewhat enjoyable, then it will fuel a positive feedback cycle in the brain. Eventually the patient will want to go to these events unprompted–and even look forward to them.

"The overarching goal is to do things that have a chance of feeling important, enjoyable or both. These activities are intended to feed on themselves," Smoski says. "For example, by being a supportive friend, their friendships become deeper, more rewarding, and it feels easier over time to set and keep those goals."

"We know that people with anhedonia don't look forward to things other people might find enjoyable, and unless they put themselves in the position to try something they won't have the opportunity to enjoy it," says Erika Forbes, a professor of psychiatry at the University of Pittsburgh who researches anhedonia but is not involved with this trial. "This is 'fake it until it becomes real'–and that can happen," she says.

The core idea of prompting patients to take external actions is what psychologists call "activation"–it is a key component of all behavioral activation interventions. The anhedonia-specific trial adds two new pieces that are not considered standard, Smoski says.

"One is what we are calling dabbling–each week trying one new thing that is a short-term commitment, just to try it. The other is practice in savoring–noticing what you like about an activity using your five senses or noticing a sense of pride or enjoyment in an accomplishment."

Targeting anhedonia directly, as opposed to treating overall depression, is a relatively new idea that is attracting increasing attention. Michelle Craske at the University of California, Los Angeles, is working on a behavioral intervention called positive affect treatment. Like the Smoski–Dichter work, it aims to beef up the brain's sensitivity to rewards but it has a greater focus on asking patients to recount recent enjoyable events in order to emphasize and reinforce pleasure. Forbes, meanwhile, is running her own multiyear study tracking teens who are at high risk of developing anhedonia to see how the condition develops during adolescence and whether it presages worse long-term outcomes in that population, as some research suggests.

"Anhedonia is a symptom that is really hard to move around from a clinical perspective, so finding out what may underlie it is really savvy," says Randy Auerbach, a professor of psychiatry at Columbia University who is not part of these studies. And because it is "a really debilitating condition" that affects such a wide range of patients well beyond those with depression, Forbes points out, the payoff of a successful treatment could be enormous.

About the Author

Dina Fine Maron, formerly an associate editor at Scientific American*, is now a wildlife trade investigative reporter at* National Geographic.

Why Exercise May Be the Best Fix for Depression

By Ferris Jabr

On Valentine's Day 2014 Jack Metta (then known as Elizabeth Droge-Young) admitted themself to a hospital in Syracuse, N.Y. For more than a year they had been struggling with depression—not eating well and losing interest in the movies, books and music that usually delighted them. They had withdrawn from friends and were routinely missing classes at Syracuse University, where they were a fifth-year graduate student in evolutionary biology. Some days that winter they could not even make it out of bed, despite the fact that they had started taking antidepressants the previous fall. In their darkest moments, obsessive and frightening thoughts of self-harm and suicide flooded their mind. "It was horrible," Metta recalls. "I felt very unsafe." They realized they needed a serious intervention.

After a week and a half on suicide watch at the hospital, plus a stronger cocktail of medications, Metta returned home, taking an academic leave of absence for the remainder of the school year. For a while they seemed to be getting better. But when they went back to school in August 2014, the unbearable sadness and dark impulses resurfaced. This time Metta turned to a hospital in Saratoga Springs, N.Y., some two and a half hours away, that offered a more holistic treatment. In addition to medication and counseling, their doctors prescribed a full schedule of daily activities such as arts and crafts and walks around the grounds. During their stay, a hospital therapist also recommended exercise. So after leaving the hospital, Metta started going to the gym three to five times a week, walking and jogging on the treadmill, lifting weights and attending Zumba, a popular dance fitness class.

"It was empowering," says Metta, now 37 and living in Denver. "It really helped with my mood. There's something wonderful about the mind-body connection exercise provides. Using weight machines or jogging on the treadmill allows you to be self-reflective: 'Look at the strength and endurance I have. This is something positive about myself.' And the dancing was joyful–just being able to move around in a way that was free and felt good." Since incorporating exercise into their regimen for managing depression, Metta has never relapsed to the point of requiring another hospitalization. To this day, they continue to incorporate movement into their daily routine as much as possible.

The fact that exercise improves physical health is so well known as to be a platitude. Decades of research demonstrate that regular exercise lowers the risk of many illnesses–heart disease, diabetes, cancer–and extends the average life span. In contrast, the benefits of exercise for mental health are not quite so obvious or well publicized. We work out to "get in shape," and some of us depend on bike rides, neighborhood jogs or yoga to help clear our mind and relieve stress. But how often do we seriously consider exercise as a viable treatment for mental illness, one just as effective as medication or counseling? Can a steady routine of physical workouts really help to keep psychological disorders in check?

In the case of depression, the collective evidence to date suggests that the answer is an emphatic yes. Exercise is by no means a panacea, and in severe cases of depression, it may be futile on its own. But scores of experiments now show that exercise is much more than a temporary distraction from mental woes or some ultimately inconsequential palliative. It appears to combat depression in a number of ways: by strengthening our biochemical resilience to stress, encouraging the growth of new brain cells, bolstering self-esteem and possibly even counterbalancing an underlying genetic risk for mental illness. For most people with mild to moderate depression, exercise is one of the strongest, safest, most practical, most affordable and even most enjoyable treatments available.

"I am a big believer in the value of physical activity," says clinical psychologist James Blumenthal of Duke University. "The majority of evidence suggests that a certain subset of patients can benefit just as much with exercise, if not more, as with medication." Psychiatrist

Madhukar Trivedi of the University of Texas Southwestern Medical Center, who has studied the relation between exercise and mental health for almost 20 years, agrees: "We have now generated a whole big body of literature about exercise as a treatment for depression. We've looked at dose, at adding exercise as an augmentation treatment, at specific biomarkers associated with improvement. We have the studies to show that something really powerful and interesting is going on."

On the Strength of the Evidence

Major depression–an illness characterized by a persistent low mood or loss of interest in typically pleasurable activities, often accompanied by insomnia, fatigue, poor concentration or feelings of worthlessness–is one of the leading causes of disability and death around the globe, according to the World Health Organization. At any given time, it afflicts around 350 million people worldwide and 18 million people in the U.S. Only a fraction of sufferers seek help, and of those, only a third respond to standard treatment, which is usually counseling and medication. Antidepressant drugs are often costly and can have serious side effects, driving many patients to search for less expensive, safer, more natural solutions. In a survey of more than 2,000 U.S. adults published in 2001, more than half of the respondents with depression said that they had turned to some kind of alternative treatment, such as yoga, herbal medicines or acupuncture.

Psychologists and clinicians have studied exercise as an alternative treatment for depression for at least 30 years. Blumenthal was one of the pioneers. In the 1980s, while researching how exercise helps patients with cardiovascular disease, he and his colleagues noticed an inadvertent secondary benefit: working out seemed to improve people's moods and reduce symptoms of depression. They decided to investigate. One of their early studies, published in 1999, tracked the health of 156 elderly men and women diagnosed with depression as they exercised regularly or took antidepressants, or both. After 16 weeks, all three groups had improved equally, but relapse rates were lowest among patients who exercised.

In a follow-up study, published a decade later, they divided more than 200 adults with depression into four groups, each receiving a different intervention: supervised exercise classes, exercise at home, medication or placebo. They found that patients engaging in supervised exercise fared better than those working out at home and achieved remission rates nearly equivalent to those of people taking antidepressants: 45 versus 47 percent, respectively. By comparison, the home exercise group reached a 40 percent remission rate and the placebo group 31 percent.

In a similar study in 2015, Swedish scientists assigned 946 patients with mild to moderate depression to one of three 12-week treatments: thrice-weekly sessions of yoga, aerobics or strength training; Internet-based cognitive-behavioral therapy; or standard counseling plus medication. Patients in all groups improved, but those engaging in exercise experienced the greatest benefits. Internet-based therapy came in as a close runner-up, but the typical treatment plan lagged behind both alternatives.

To date, numerous meta-analyses have kept score on the accumulating data. They do not all agree: a few have found no indication that exercise is helpful or have found that it offers only very small effects or greatly diminished benefits in the long term. But most have reached similar optimistic conclusions. A 2013 review by the nonprofit organization Cochrane, regarded as a leader in evidence-based medicine, concluded that exercise is just as effective a treatment for depression as medication and counseling.

A meta-analysis published in 2016 echoes Cochrane's finding. A team of international researchers examined 25 of the most rigorous experiments and determined that exercise, especially moderate to vigorous aerobic exercise under professional supervision, is indeed a potent treatment for depression. When they adjusted their analysis to account for weak studies—those most prone to some kind of experimental bias—they found an even stronger effect, suggesting that some previous meta-analyses may have underestimated exercise's benefits for mental health. The researchers further calculated that it would take at least 1,000 contradictory studies to negate the affirming evidence that has piled up so far. Yet another review computed that when exercise is used to treat depression, success rates increase by as much as 67 to 74 percent.

How Much Is Enough?

Some researchers have attempted to figure out what types of exercise and intensity levels are most effective as an antidepressant. In a frequently cited study from 2005, for example, Trivedi and his colleagues tracked the health of 80 adults with mild to moderate depression for three months as they exercised three to five times a week on a treadmill or stationary bicycle at low intensity (seven kilocalories per kilogram per week) or at a higher intensity, as recommended by public health authorities (17.5 kilocalories per kilogram per week). At the end of the three months, the adults who exercised at the higher intensity had lessened the severity of their depression by 47 percent, compared with only 30 percent for the low-intensity group and 29 percent for a group who engaged in stretching rather than aerobic exercise.

On the basis of studies such as this one, some psychologists, clinicians and health authorities have gone as far as publishing specific recommendations. Trivedi prescribes three to five 45- to 60-minute sessions of aerobic exercise (walking; running; cycling; or using a treadmill, stationary bike or elliptical trainer) each week at an intensity of 50 to 85 percent of maximum heart rate. "The ideal is probably at least 16 kilocalories per kilogram of body weight, which works out to 1,200 to 1,500 kilocalories each week for average body weight," Trivedi says. "If you can talk to your spouse on the phone, you're not working out at the right intensity."

Likewise Central Queensland University exercise psychologist Robert Stanton advises 30- to 40-minute sessions of aerobic exercise—walking, cross-training or stationary cycling—three to four times a week at low to moderate intensity for at least nine weeks. And the

U.K. National Institute for Health and Care Excellence advocates group-based physical activity programs for patients with mild to moderate depression consisting of at least three 45-minute sessions a week for at least 10 weeks.

Other experts, however, think it may be too soon to get so specific. A 2013 review paper, for instance, concluded that both cardiovascular and resistance exercise, either alone or in combination, are effective at treating depression but that there are not yet enough data to definitively favor one form of physical activity over another.

"Which exercise has the best mood effects, and what intensity is best? Does it work better alone or combined with other treatments? We don't know for certain yet," says psychologist Michael Otto of Boston University, who has studied both the emotional and cognitive benefits of exercise. "We can make some general suggestions, but we still need more data to be confident about the specifics."

Why Exercise Works

In the past two decades scientists have uncovered numerous details about how exercise alters the brain, and the body as a whole, in ways that alleviate and protect against depression. The second you start running, pedaling or lifting a dumbbell, your body's chemistry begins to change. Exercise boosts your heart rate, sending blood, oxygen, hormones and neurochemicals surging through the body. In the moment, the body responds to exercise as a kind of stress–but it is ultimately beneficial. Some evidence suggests that habitual moderate exercise rewires the brain and immune system to better cope with physical and mental strain. The better the body becomes at dealing with stressors of all kinds, the lower the risk of a depressive episode. In fact, many researchers think of depression as a disorder of managing stress.

Exercise also seems to mimic some of the chemical effects of antidepressant medication. Based on increasing evidence, some scientists argue that certain cases of depression result from the impaired growth of both brain cells and the connections between them. Studies have documented the atrophy and loss of neurons in brain regions such as the amygdala, hippocampus and prefrontal cortex in patients with major depression. Antidepressants that increase levels of serotonin and other neurotransmitters might work by reinvigorating neural proliferation, a process that depends in part on a molecule called brain-derived neurotrophic factor (BDNF). In studies with both animals and people, exercise enhances the production of BDNF.

In one 2001 study, for example, rats given an antidepressant and the opportunity to run produced higher levels of BDNF compared with animals that only ran or only received medication. Moreover, they were better at enduring a stressful experience, swimming for longer in an inescapable water tank before giving up—a test designed to approximate the onset of depression. In an analogous human study in 2016, researchers in Brazil divided 57 adults taking the antidepressant sertraline for moderate to severe depression into two groups: one attended four sessions of aerobic activity a week for 28 days, and the other did not exercise. Symptoms abated similarly in both groups, but the exercise group improved on lower doses of antidepressants. The authors suspect that exercise enhanced the biochemical effects of the drugs. Similar studies have shown that simply recommending healthy lifestyle changes, such as establishing better sleep routines and getting more exercise, can dramatically boost the efficacy of antidepressants from a mere 10 percent remission rate with the drugs alone to a 60 percent remission rate.

And in a small but intriguing 2015 study, physician Helmuth Haslacher and his colleagues at the Medical University of Vienna in Austria compared the mental health and genomes of 55 elderly marathon runners and endurance bicyclists with those of 58 nonathletes. Among the nonathletes, they found a statistically significant correlation between the number of depressive symptoms these individuals experienced and a particular gene variant that interferes with normal BDNF production. Among the athletes, however, there was no such correlation. The researchers concluded that by stimulating BDNF production, long-term, vigorous aerobic exercise might actually counteract a genetic susceptibility to depression.

Neurobiology may also explain why, in addition to exercise countering depression, the inverse seems to be true: correlations in epidemiological surveys suggest that physical inactivity, while sometimes the result of depression, may also be a major risk factor for subsequently developing it. In a 2014 study of more than 6,000 elderly U.K. citizens, the more time people spent watching television, the more likely they were to report symptoms of depression (although this was not true for other sedentary activities such as reading). Those who participated in some form of vigorous physical activity at least once a week experienced less depression. Likewise, a 2015 survey of nearly 5,000 Chinese college students found that the more time a student spent in front of a TV or computer screen, the more likely he or she was to have depressive symptoms. In contrast, the risk for depression dropped the more physically active a student was, regardless of age, gender or residential background. A meta-analysis of 24 studies involving a total of nearly 200,000 participants reached the same conclusion: sedentary behavior was associated with an increased risk of depression. On average, active people are 45 percent less likely to be depressed than inactive people, according to the U.S. Office of Disease Prevention and Health Promotion.

The Feel-Good Factor

Beyond these physiological reasons, many social and psychological factors help to explain why working out can alleviate symptoms of depression. In comprehensive interviews, people who have struggled with the disorder say that exercise energizes them, gives them a sense of purpose and achievement, elevates their self-esteem and mood, regulates appetite and sleep cycles, and distracts them from negative thoughts. For those who exercise in a group, it can also provide a welcome opportunity for social interaction.

First, though, many people with depression must overcome a severe lack of motivation. "We need to educate people and give them tools to help monitor their progress," Trivedi says. "We make patients log in and communicate with us. If we find out they have skipped a day, we work with them to solve the problem and make sure that by the end of week, they complete their regimen."

Jennifer Carter, director of sport psychology at the Ohio State University Wexner Medical Center, has come up with a bevy of practical tips. Among them: "Notice the facts," she advises. "For example, there are 1,440 minutes in a day. Perhaps you can find 30 of those to exercise."

Getting over that initial hurdle of low motivation seems to depend in particular on how much satisfaction and self-agency people experience while working out. "Enjoyment is fundamentally linked to how much people stick with exercise," Otto says. "I want them to do what is most fun and entertaining, whatever that might be." Research suggests that exercise as therapy succeeds when people choose the type and intensity. Most people prefer a moderate intensity, around or just below the ventilatory threshold–the point at which breathing becomes noticeably labored. In 2011 Patrick Callaghan, now at London South Bank University in England, and his colleagues asked 38 women with depression to exercise on treadmills in small groups three times a week, at either a prescribed intensity or one they personally selected. After a month, the women who chose how much to exert themselves had lower levels of depression and higher self-esteem compared with the other group.

Despite the mounting evidence that exercise can remedy some forms of depression, skepticism persists in academia and health care, Trivedi notes. "There is this general bias that exercise is not a bona fide treatment–it's just something you should do in addition to treatment, like trying to sleep and eat well," he says. "Even though recognition of exercise as a treatment is increasing," only some health insurance companies pay for gym time, he explains, and when they do, they often offer small temporary discounts. "I can prescribe a drug that costs $200 and insurance will pay, but they won't give $40 to open a gym membership."

Patients will need to change their thinking as well. "It can be hard for patients to think of exercise as a form of treatment," Otto comments. "We usually exercise to look good at the beach, to lose weight." Most individuals do not understand the degree to which exercise can reshape their mood, too. "Even if you feel like pulling in and doing nothing, exercise pushes you out," he adds. "Depression makes you feel like everything you're about to do is useless and pointless. That's exactly what exercise fights–you have to get up and go."

About the Author

Ferris Jabr is a contributing writer for Scientific American. *He has also written for the* New York Times Magazine, *the* New Yorker *and* Outside.

Mindfulness Can Improve Your Attention and Health

By Amishi P. Jha

Pulling into a parking spot at work, you realize you have no recollection of the drive that got you there. While reading a news story, you arrive at the bottom of the page, frustrated that you have no idea what you just read. In midconversation you suddenly become aware that you have missed what the person speaking to you has said.

These episodes are symptoms of a distracted mind. You were thinking about a project idea while driving, reliving a troubling memory while attempting to read, envisioning a weekend getaway with friends during a conversation with your co-worker. Whether the mind journeyed to the future or to the past, whether the thoughts that whisked you away were useful, unpleasant or pleasant, the consequences were the same. You missed the experience of the moment as it was unfolding. Your mind drifted into mental time travel.

Away from the Now

Mental time travel evolved to advantage our survival. By reexperiencing the past, we can learn from it, and by preexperiencing the future, we can prepare for it. Both *retro*spection (rewinding events in the mind) and *pro*spection (fast-forwarding them) rely on our brain's capacity for mental simulation. And based on the brain nodes and networks that carry out simulation, chief among them regions of the prefrontal cortex, we can glean that this is a recently gained evolutionary development. How does mental simulation work, and what does it have to do with stress and mind wandering (which is distinct from deliberate daydreaming)?

Before we discuss that, let's test our simulation abilities. Imagine being handed a delicious chocolate cupcake with creamy white frosting. You lift it up to your mouth, anticipating the rich chocolate flavor. But as you go to take a bite, I inform you that the frosting is made of cod-liver oil and cauliflower. The likely response: Yuck!

Let's break down what happened. The initial description of the cupcake prompted a mental image in your mind, and your attention transported you into a simulated experience, perhaps so vivid that you could almost taste the cupcake and feel your mouth watering. You recoiled as soon as you "pretasted" the seemingly disgusting cod-liver oil concoction.

Simulations have the power to transport our attention out of the present moment while simultaneously altering our cognitive, emotional and physiological responses in the now. The same mental powers that drove up your salivary response when you "previewed" a cupcake can drive down your mood, focus and thinking if you preview a threatening episode over and over. Worse, they can stimulate the pituitary gland to release more stress hormones. Herein lies the downside of this evolutionary advance: as our attention journeys to an alternative reality, our mind and body respond as if that reality were unfolding in the here and now.

Research suggests that this type of mental meandering away from our present moment has many deleterious consequences for our minds, bodies and relationships. Such mind wandering can spike during stressful times in our lives, be they acute or chronic events. And as mind wandering increases in the form of more frequent rumination or worrying, our experience of stress expands, creating a spiral of thinking that reduces our concentration while increasing our levels of stress hormones.

In my laboratory at the University of Miami, we study the human brain's attention system. To investigate whether and how stress influences attention, we partner with people in some of the most extreme, high-demand lines of work: medical professionals, firefighters, soldiers and elite athletes. They need to deploy their attention—and do it well—in extraordinarily high-stakes circumstances where their decisions could impact many people. One group we have worked with extensively is the U.S. military. Whether and how people in this demographic pay attention can be a matter of life or death. For all of us, attention is a powerful force that shapes our lives far more than we realize.

Our attention influences our perceptual, emotional, decisional and social functioning and therefore affects our sense of fulfillment and accomplishment. Many of our participants experience protracted high-stress intervals, such as soldiers enduring predeployment training or military deployment, and we wondered what happens to attention over these intervals. We learned that, similar to what is observed in lab-based studies, experiencing stress in the field indeed causes attentional performance to decline while increasing mind wandering. This prompted the next important question: Can attention be trained to resist stress-related increases in mind wandering?

My group first considered mindfulness training as a potential solution in the early 2000s. If mentally zooming into the past or future was the root cause of "attentional hijacking," then perhaps the most effective antidote would be a training regimen that emphasized a present-centered attentional stance.

Antidote to a Wandering Mind

The opposite of a wandering mind is a mindful one. Mindfulness is a mental mode characterized by attention to the present moment without evaluation or emotional reaction to it. Eastern cultures have proffered various forms of meditation as a solution to the conundrum of human suffering. Ancient texts detail precise training exercises to cultivate specific mental qualities. One form of meditation, which we now call mindfulness meditation, instructs practitioners to pay attention to ongoing perceptual experience rather than conceptual trains of thought. People have been engaging in mindfulness exercises for millennia, claiming improved mental clarity and calm–and even greater longevity.

Thousands of articles lay out evidence that training to become more mindful reduces psychological stress and improves both mental and physical health, alleviating depression, anxiety, loneliness and chronic pain [*see "Capturing Attention" below*]. Many workplaces and medical centers now offer mindfulness-based programs to improve well-being. There has been an explosive proliferation of mindfulness training modalities beyond this as well, from apps and asynchronous online trainings to trainer-led in-person and remote programs.

One broad category of mindfulness exercises is focused-attention practices. These practices guide individuals to select a specific sensation tied to, for example, breathing and direct attention to that sensation. Instructions next encourage the practitioner to notice when his or her mind has wandered away from that attentional target and, when mind wandering is registered, to simply return attention back to the immediate breath-related sensations.

A second category emphasizes receptive-attention practices, which coach practitioners to engage in open monitoring. They are to watch what enters and then drops out of conscious awareness moment by moment. Think of hearing the faint sound of a fire truck's siren in the distance. The sound becomes louder as the truck approaches, then fainter again as it passes. You may notice that the siren is initially part of a vast sea of sounds and later the most salient sound, only to fade into the background again. Thoughts, emotions and other sensations may similarly grow and diminish as we remain in a watchful monitoring mode.

One of the best-studied mindfulness training programs was developed by Jon Kabat-Zinn of the University of Massachusetts Medical School in the late 1970s. The program, called mindfulness-based stress reduction (MBSR), introduces participants to both these broad categories of exercise. It is offered over eight weeks and involves weekly group meetings with a qualified trainer, as well as daily homework practices of 45 minutes a day.

As its name highlights, MBSR aims to promote stress reduction, as well as treatment for those suffering from any one of myriad ailments. The application and reach of MBSR have mushroomed over the past decade, and it has guided many mindfulness-based interventions (MBIs) designed to improve the health of the body, the mind and relationships. These practices have been shown to alleviate stress-related inflammatory and cardiovascular diseases, as well as psychological disorders and diseases such as anxiety and depression. In addition, several studies report that MBIs improve interpersonal dynamics and team cohesion in the workplace.

Training Attention

From a clinical perspective, although the field is admittedly in its infancy, the evidence is promising regarding the somatic, psychological and social benefits of mindfulness training. Yet my interest is from a cognitive neuroscience perspective: If mindfulness does work, how does it work? A review of mindfulness training exercises showed that they certainly highlight attention, but they also emphasize the detection of mind wandering. We needed to put mindfulness to the test in a manner that would allow us to assess both these components.

To do this, we used the "sustained attention to response" task, or SART. This test was developed in the late 1990s, and, as the name suggests, it tests a person's ability to sustain attention. Participants sit in front of a computer screen where a number appears for half a second and then vanishes. A half-second later, another number appears and then vanishes, and so on for 20 minutes. Their job: press the space bar every time a number appears–*unless* the number is three. By design, the number three appears only 5 percent of the time.

This test engages the three main subsystems of attention: orienting, or directing attention; alerting, or noticing events; and executive attention, or managing goals and performance. You orient attention to the screen, focusing on each number as it flickers; stay alert for the appearance of the number three; and use executive attention to make sure you are following the instructions and pressing the key only when you should.

It sounds simple, but it is not easy. Most participants do not perform well on this task. Why? They quickly go on autopilot, lost in their own mental simulations, and press the space bar no matter what number appears. Their attention goes off task. We know this because we stopped the experiment and asked them every now and then. Their minds wandered numerous times throughout the experiment, and during those episodes, their performance suffered compared with when they stayed on task.

We have used this experiment in many studies to see whether mindfulness training strengthens attention and reduces mind wandering in individuals experiencing intervals of high demand such as an academic semester or military deployment. We found that for a variety of groups ranging from undergraduate students to elite military units, mindfulness training indeed benefited SART performance. Compared with those who received no training, those in the mindfulness training groups had higher SART accuracy scores and less mind wandering over time.

In a 2020 study published in the *Journal of Cognitive Enhancement*, Frederikke Piil, then at the University of Southern Denmark, and her colleagues examined the consequences of acute stress and mindfulness training on SART performance in 48 university students and staff members. All participants were provided with one of two apps that required their engagement in daily practices over an interval of one month. One group used a mindfulness app to practice mindfulness exercises, and the other group used a cognitive training app to complete simple cognitive exercises.

To determine a baseline at the start of the experiment, participants first completed a cold pressor task–they submerged their nondominant hand in a tank of circulating ice water until it became too uncomfortable to keep it there. This task has been found to reliably increase stress as measured by increases in arousal of the sympathetic nervous system (for example, increased heart rate, blood pressure and stress hormones). Afterward they completed the SART. They returned a month later and once again completed the cold pressor task followed by the SART. Only the mindfulness group improved in their SART performance, and the more they used the mindfulness app, the more their performance benefited.

Because attention and mind wandering are known to correspond with academic performance, Clemens C. Bauer of the Massachusetts Institute of Technology and his colleagues used the SART test in combination with brain imaging in school-aged children. In their study, published in 2020 in *Human Brain Mapping*, half of 99 sixth graders received mindfulness training, and the other half received a computer-coding course.

After training, only the mindfulness group demonstrated preserved SART performance over the demanding academic semester. This group showed increased anticorrelation between activity in the central executive network, a key brain network for attention, and activity in the default mode network, known to be activated during mental simulations and mind wandering. Greater anticorrelation between these two networks after training indicates that only members of the mindfulness group improved in their cognitive control. These results suggest that mindfulness training may help children to stay focused and complete the task at hand.

Interestingly, recent work by Lukas Lenhart of the Medical University of Innsbruck in Austria and his colleagues in which participants received seven weeks of mindfulness training revealed altered brain structure in specific nodes tied to attention and mind wandering. In that study, published in 2020 in *Behavioural Brain Research*, 27 participants received an MRI scan before and after the mindfulness course. The researchers observed increased gray matter density in subjects' frontal lobe nodes within attentional networks, as well as decreases in gray matter density within nodes of the default mode.

Together these studies suggest that mindfulness training may provide a type of mental armor during times of protracted and acute stress and can serve to boost focus. It appears to benefit both children and adults, resulting in functional and structural brain changes. Such training allows us to break free from a wandering mind that can distract us from the task at hand and sour our mood. With our full capacity available to us, all aspects of our functioning that are fueled by attention will benefit, be it our ability to think, feel or connect.

Prescription For the Brain

Efforts to become more mindful could make a considerable dent in human suffering. Working mindfulness practices into your daily routine may bring benefits similar to those of physical exercise. Indeed, as with physical exercise, mindfulness exercises are stress-protective, and the more you do, the more you benefit. As an antidote to an ambling mind, negative mood and stress, such mental workouts may have the potential to help virtually everyone live a happier, healthier and more fulfilled life. Students or athletes who want to boost their performance, for example, and parents, teachers or caregivers wishing to be more attentive to others' needs may all find mindfulness training useful. Such training may be particularly essential, however, for soldiers, first responders, critical care nurses and physicians, and air-traffic controllers, whose ability to control and monitor their attention may be a matter of life or death.

A key insight from our research is that merely learning about the damaging effects of stress or the benefits, history or mechanisms of mindfulness training did not lead to attentional improvements. Only engaging in regular mindfulness practice did. In studies across military service members and athletes, among others, we found a dose-response effect; the more practice people engaged in, the more they benefited. But conversely, we also found that when we assigned 30 minutes of daily practice, most time-pressured participants simply did not comply. Some did the 30 minutes; others did none. We pursued this "dosing question" across several studies to arrive at a daily practice prescription to which participants were willing to adhere: 12 to 15 minutes a day five days a week. When this group followed through, we saw beneficial effects on their attention. The research continues, and many more studies will be required.

With evidence of its benefits mounting come new challenges for mindfulness training. How can access be scaled up *and* meet the needs of specific groups? Based on our past research, my colleague Scott Rogers and I created a short-form program called mindfulness-based attention training (MBAT). Once we found the core program to be effective, we developed train-the-trainer methods to address scalability challenges. MBAT's modular structure and exercises allow for flexibility so the program can be customized for a variety of groups, from soldiers to medical students, athletes, business professionals, first responders and teachers. The linchpin of the program's success is the competency of the trainers. We are finding that more so than prior expertise in mindfulness, successful trainers must have familiarity with the cultural norms, sensitivities and stressors that a particular community faces.

The scientific literature on mindfulness training is still in its infancy, and many scientists are calling for more rigorous research methods such as standardized programs and better placebo-controlled designs. Yet the promise of mindfulness continues to generate much interest. The overarching message seems to be that the more time spent engaging in such training, the more benefits in attention. No matter our profession, as we learn to grab hold of our attention and become more meta-aware of our moment-to-moment experience, we gain the power to intervene in support of our own happiness and health.

About the Author

Amishi P. Jha, author of the book Peak Mind *(HarperOne, October 2021), is a professor of psychology at the University of Miami, where she serves as director of contemplative neuroscience for the Mindfulness Research and Practice Initiative. Her research investigates the neural bases of attention, resilience and mindfulness.*

Evolution Could Explain Why Psychotherapy May Work for Depression

By Gary Stix

A consensus has emerged in recent years that psychotherapies–in particular, cognitive behavioral therapy (CBT)–rate comparably to medications such as Prozac and Lexapro as treatments for depression. Either option, or the two together, may at times alleviate the mood disorder. In looking more closely at both treatments, CBT–which delves into dysfunctional thinking patterns–may have a benefit that could make it the better choice for a patient.

The reason may be rooted in our deep evolutionary past. Scholars suggest humans may become depressed to help us focus attention on a problem that might cause someone to fall out of step with family, friends, clan or the larger society–an outcast status that, especially in Paleolithic times, would have meant an all-but-certain tragic fate. Depression, by this account, came about as a mood state to make us think long and hard about behaviors that may have caused us to become despondent because some issue in our lives is socially problematic.

A recent article in *American Psychologist*, the flagship publication of the American Psychological Association, weighs what the possible evolutionary origins of depression might mean for arguments about the merits of psychotherapy versus antidepressants. In the article, Steven D. Hollon, a professor of psychology at Vanderbilt University, explores the implications of helping a patient come to grips with the underlying causes of a depression–which is the goal of CBT, and is also in line with an evolutionary explanation. The anodyne effects of an antidepressant, by contrast, may divert a patient from engaging in the reflective process for which depression evolved–a reason perhaps that psychotherapy appears to produce a more enduring effect than antidepressants. *Scientific American* spoke with Hollon about his ideas on the topic.

[An edited transcript of the interview follows].

Q: You described in your recent article the idea that humans evolved a propensity toward depression as a means to restore emotional and psychological equilibrium. That allows people to stay well integrated within their social milieus. So, can you explain how depression may be a product of evolution that can actually protect us?

A: In the late 2000s, I read a paper by the evolutionary biologist Paul Andrews. It was masterful, very thoughtful–and I totally disagreed with it. The main premise was that depression was an evolved adaptation that serves to make people ruminate.

Q: Why did you disagree?

A: For clinicians, we think of rumination as a terrible thing that at best is a symptom of depression and at worst leads to something that deepens the depression. We've always thought of it as a kind of exhaust out the tailpipe that is not really helpful.

But the work of Andrews and his colleague J. Andrew (Andy) Thomson recounted that in our evolutionary past, what got you depressed was some kind of major problem–probably a social problem–that might get you excluded from the tribe. And what you had to do is sit down and think about things.

Most of us can think of anxiety as being a useful function, because anxiety takes us away from danger. It's quick, it's rapid, the reaction that occurs after stepping on a snake that might be poisonous when you're out in the woods. But most folks don't think of depression as having any function. It's just something unpleasant. The trick is to figure out what the purpose of depression is–and when Andrews and Thomson looked at what goes on when you get depressed, they found that a lot of energy went to the brain.

And the reason for that is to help us to think more carefully about the things that are going wrong, and first to understand what's the cause. That answers the question: How come I'm feeling so bad? And the second thing is: How can I do a good job of figuring out a solution to a problem?

So, you don't have to move rapidly in depression; the bad thing has already happened. You don't have to get out of the way of a poisonous snake or a leopard. But you do have to solve some kind of complex social problem, and rumination is what gets you there. So as opposed to being an unpleasant byproduct of being depressed, rumination is actually the reason why depression evolved. And it helps you solve complex social problems.

Q: You seem to now be giving some credence to the ideas of Andrews and Thomson. How does this line of thinking actually play out in people's lives? At what point does depression and the social problems that need to be ruminated upon begin?

A: These complex social problems often gear up in adolescence when young people start to ask: Am I going to have a boyfriend and girlfriend? How do I get a boy or girl to like me? Am I going to do okay in school? Are my parents happy with me? Am I going to get to go to college? Will I be able to find a job?

Q: How does your expertise in psychotherapy—and specifically cognitive behavioral therapy—jibe with the evolutionary theory of depression?

A: Cognitive therapy in this context becomes a bit of a natural. It teaches people how to ruminate more effectively. Cognitive theory holds that people got depressed because they hold inaccurate beliefs about themselves. This can be combined with the additional notion that people can get stuck. For example, if something bad happens, you start thinking that you're a failure, you're a loser. For most people, depression motivates them to think more deliberately about the causes of their problems and the solutions they can apply. In most instances in our ancestral past this worked well enough; most depressions remit spontaneously even in the absence of treatment. Cognitive therapy, at the least, hurries the process along and, at the most, helps unstick that subset of individuals who get stuck making negative ascriptions about themselves, typically about personal competence or lovability.

The solution is to essentially teach them the scientific method so they get unstuck. We ask a patient to ask themselves: what do you think is the cause of the problem? What other explanations could there be? What's the evidence supporting one or the other? And especially we encourage patients who get stuck to pit what are called their stable trait theories–"I am incompetent" or "I am unlovable"– against a more behavioral explanation: "I chose the wrong strategies."

Q: One area that you've worked on is whether CBT has a more enduring effect than drugs, and you're interested in how that might provide evidence for the evolutionary basis for depression.

A: Basically, we have good clinical evidence that cognitive therapy is at least as effective as medications in the short run, and more enduring in the long run. CBT may get people thinking carefully about their problems in a way that facilitates coming to a resolution, whereas medications may just anesthetize the stress that underlies a depression.

Q: Are you going to test that idea in some way?

A: I've got colleagues in Vietnam, where they're quite interested in a study we want to do in which we compare folks treated to recovery with CBT versus folks treated to recovery with medication– and compare those against a control that uses Chinese herbal medicine, which is widely believed there to be effective. And if it's really the case that antidepressant medications suppress symptoms in a way that worsens the underlying course of depression, then those patients should be more likely to have recurrences when we take them off the medications than when we take them off the Chinese herbal medicine. If it's really true that CBT truly has an enduring effect that protects against depression, then patients treated to recovery should be less likely to recur following treatment termination than patients who recover on Chinese herbal medicine. In essence, the Chinese herbal medicine serves as an ideal nonspecific control because it provides neither the coping skills taught in cognitive therapy nor the pharmacologically active serotonin-related ingredient provided by antidepressant medications. We have a trial that we want to do that should answer the question, but it hasn't yet been done.

Q: Doesn't some evidence exist along these lines already, though?

A: There are over half a dozen studies that indicate that patients treated to remission with cognitive therapy are less likely to relapse following treatment termination than patients treated to remission with antidepressant medications–and a pair of studies that suggest that this enduring effect may extend to the prevention of recurrence. What we do not know is where all this fits within the proposed evolutionary context: whether cognitive therapy has an enduring effect, or antidepressant medications may be detrimental in terms of prolonging the life of the underlying episode–as evolutionary theory suggests. What is needed is a nonspecific control that neither has enduring effects or the anesthetizing effects caused by the medication. Whether cognitive therapy truly has an enduring effect, or antidepressant medications have a detrimental effect, remains to be determined. The comparison of each to a nonspecific control like Chinese herbal medicine should allow us to determine in absolute terms which is which.

Q: You've talked about the difficulties in trying to measure whether there really are enduring effects in this type of trial.

A: It also is possible that the enduring effects observed for cognitive therapy (relative to antidepressant medications) have to do with changes that occur during the course of a clinical trial.

Although we randomize patients to cognitive therapy versus antidepressant medications at the outset of the trial, we typically lose about 15 percent of the sample because of attrition, and another 25 percent as a nonresponse to either intervention. That means that only about 60 percent of the sample initially randomized makes it into the comparison of subsequent rates of relapse. If different kinds of patients remit to cognitive therapy than to antidepressant medications, that could bias any subsequent comparisons.

Q: Do you think that these insights about CBT could have an impact for severe depression?

A: I don't know, and wouldn't necessarily assume that they would. For psychotic depression, you'd go to electroconvulsive therapy first. I'm not sure that the analytical rumination hypothesis will apply to psychotic depressions, or that it needs to. For every evolved adaptation there are instances in which the mechanism evolved breaks down and the condition can be considered to be an actual disease or disorder.

About the Author

Gary Stix is a senior editor at Scientific American.

The Best Diet for Your Brain

By Bret Stetka

Carolyn feels great these days. She exercises. She's socially active. She spends as much time with her four grandchildren as possible. But it wasn't always that way. A retired radiology film librarian from Pittsburgh, she began feeling apathetic and isolated seven years ago. "I'd just lost my mother, and my two sons had moved away," recalls Carolyn, now 75. She also struggled with excess weight, diabetes and chronic lung disease. She was grieving, eating a worrisome amount of junk food and slipping into what looked a lot like depression.

A few years later a friend told Carolyn about a depression-prevention study at the University of Pittsburgh. She signed up immediately. All 247 participants were, like her, older adults with mild depressive symptoms—people who without treatment face a 20 to 25 percent chance of succumbing to major depression. Half received about five hours of problem-solving therapy, a cognitive-behavioral approach designed to help patients cope with stressful life experiences. The rest, including Carolyn, received dietary counseling. Guided by a social worker, she discovered that she liked salmon, tuna and a number of other "brain-healthy" foods—which quickly replaced all the chips, cake and candy she was eating.

When the trial concluded in 2014, the results came as a surprise—to the researchers at least. The dietary counseling was not meant to have any substantial effect; Carolyn's group was the experiment's control. And yet psychiatrist Charles Reynolds and his colleagues discovered that both interventions had significantly reduced the risk of depression—by approximately the same amount. When they reviewed the data, all the patients scored on average 40 to 50 percent lower on the Beck Depression Inventory test, a common measure of depressive symptoms, 15 months after their sessions ended. What is more, only about 8 percent, regardless of the therapy they received, had fallen into major depression.

It cannot be ruled out that a placebo effect contributed to the improvements seen in both groups. Meeting with a health care professional and being proactive about getting better in and of itself may have helped participants feel more upbeat. In Carolyn's view, however, she had reversed her downward spiral largely by changing how she ate.

She is not alone in making that connection. Among scientists and clinicians there is a growing appreciation of the critical interplay between diet and brain health. The evidence is preliminary, and it is hard to tease out cause and effect. Perhaps people who eat well are also apt to have other healthy brain habits, such as regular exercise and good sleep routines. Or maybe depressed people tend to self-medicate with Oreos. But the data continue to accumulate. Every year the list of correlations between certain foods and mental well-being grows: fish and other sources of omega-3 fatty acids might help fend off psychosis and depression; fermented foods such as yogurt, pickles and sauerkraut seem to ease anxiety; green tea and antioxidant-rich fruits may help keep dementia at bay. And so on.

There is probably no single ingredient, no happy seed from the jungles of beyond, that is sure to secure a better mood or mental acuity into old age. But there do appear to be specific dietary patterns—calibrated by millions of years of human evolution—that boost our cognitive and psychological fitness. Within the nascent field of nutritional psychiatry, consensus is building about just what types of diets are best. And perhaps most exciting is the prospect that dietary intervention could serve as a valuable adjunct to medication and other therapies for mental disorders—just as it does in so many other areas of medicine.

Good Diet, Bad Diet

When it comes to promoting brain health, the diet supported by the strongest data draws on traditional eating patterns from Italy, Greece and Spain. The so-called Mediterranean diet consists primarily of fruits, vegetables, nuts, whole grains, fish, lean meats in moderation, olive oil and maybe a little red wine. Earlier this year the first-ever randomized controlled clinical trial to test a prescribed diet to treat depression was published in *BMC Medicine*. The "SMILES" trial reported that after 12 weeks of consuming a Mediterranean-like diet, patients suffering from moderate to severe depression experienced significantly greater improvements on a commonly used depression symptom measure called the Montgomery-Åsberg Depression Rating scale (MADRS), compared with the control group. In 2011 public health expert Almudena Sánchez-Villegas of the University of Las Palmas de Gran Canaria and her colleagues assessed the relation between this diet and depression in more than 12,000 healthy Spaniards over the course of a median of six years each. They found that compared with people who did not eat a Mediterranean diet, those who did were significantly less likely to succumb to depression. For the subjects who followed the diet most closely, the risk dropped by a substantial 30 percent.

Sánchez-Villegas later confirmed the association in another large trial. The PREDIMED (Prevention with Mediterranean Diet) study–a multicenter research project evaluating nearly 7,500 men and women across Spain–initially looked at whether a Mediterranean diet, supplemented with extra nuts, protects against cardiovascular disease. It does. But in 2013 Sánchez-Villegas and other investigators also analyzed depression data among PREDIMED's participants. Again, compared with subjects who ate a generic low-fat diet, those who adhered to the nut-enriched Mediterranean diet had a lower risk for depression. This was especially true among people with diabetes, who saw a 40 percent drop in risk. Perhaps these patients, who cannot adequately process glucose, benefited the most because the Mediterranean diet minimized their sugar intake.

Indeed, a central feature of the diet is that it is low in sugar, as well as processed foods and fatty meats, which are commonplace on most Western menus. Nutritional psychiatry researcher and SMILES trial lead author Felice N. Jacka of Deakin University and the University of Melbourne in Australia was one of the first to demonstrate an association between stereotypical Western diets and depression and anxiety. Most recently, she has drawn another link between poor diet and, quite literally, a shrinking brain. In September 2015 she and her colleagues discovered that older adults who consumed a Western diet for four years not only suffered higher rates of mood disorders but also had a significantly smaller left hippocampus on MRI scans. The hippocampus, composed of two seahorse-shaped arcs of brain tissue deep underneath our temples, is critical to memory formation. Jacka focused on the hippocampus because animal studies have also noted diet-related changes there.

Scientists have proposed a number of possible mechanisms to explain this damage. Jacka's findings parallel other research revealing that high-sugar diets can prompt runaway inflammation and trigger a cascade of other metabolic changes that ultimately impair brain function. Ordinarily inflammation is part of our immune system's arsenal to fight infection and encourage healing, but when it is misdirected or overly aggressive, it can destroy healthy tissues as well. According to numerous studies, inflammation plays a role in a range of brain disorders—from depression and bipolar disorder to possibly autism, schizophrenia and Alzheimer's disease.

Two meta-analyses from 2010 and 2012 collectively reviewed data from 53 studies and reported significantly elevated levels of several blood markers of inflammation in depressed patients. And numerous studies have reported increased or altered activity of immune cells called microglia—which play a key role in the brain's inflammatory response—in patients with psychiatric disorders, including depression and schizophrenia. It is not clear whether inflammation causes mental illness in some cases, or vice versa. But the evidence suggests that many if not most known risk factors for psychiatric disorders, especially depression, promote inflammation; these include abuse, stress, grief and certain genetic predilections.

Jacka's work repeatedly points to traditional diets such as Mediterranean, Japanese and Scandinavian ones—all of which tend to be noninflammatory—as being best for our neurological and mental health. "There is no doubt that stress and uncomfortable emotions can cause us to reach for the biscuit tin—they don't call them comfort foods for nothing!" she admits. "But consistently the data show that the main constituents of a healthy brain diet include fruits, vegetables, legumes, nuts, fish, lean meats and healthy fats such as olive oil."

Brain-Building Fatty Acids

Increasingly, researchers are finding that the power of these more traditional diets extends beyond just supplanting bad food with good. In the summer of 2015 neuroscientists Amandine Pelletier, Christine Barul, Catherine Féart and their colleagues, all then at the University of Bordeaux in France, discovered that a Mediterranean diet may actually help physically preserve neuronal connections in the brain. They used a highly sensitive neuroimaging analysis technique called voxel-based morphometry to identify subtle changes in brain anatomy over time. And in September 2015 nutritional epidemiologist Martha C. Morris of Rush University and her co-workers reported that the MIND diet–a hybrid of the Mediterranean and the high-nutrient, low-salt DASH diet–may help slow cognitive decline and possibly even help prevent Alzheimer's. When they tested cognitive ability in 960 older adults, those who had followed the MIND diet for roughly five years achieved scores matching those of people 7.5 years younger.

Our evolutionary backstory could explain these neuroprotective effects. Sometime between 195,000 and 125,000 years ago, humans may have nearly gone extinct. A glacial period had set in that probably left much of the earth icy and barren for 70,000 years. The population of our hominin ancestors plummeted to possibly only a few hundred in number, and most experts agree that everyone alive today is descended from this group. Exactly how they–or early modern humans, for that matter–managed to stay alive during recurring glacial periods is less clear. But as terrestrial resources dried up, foraging for marine life in reliable shellfish beds surrounding Africa most likely became essential for survival. Graduate student Jan De Vynck of Nelson Mandela Metropolitan University in South Africa has shown that one person working those shellfish beds can harvest a staggering 4,500 calories an hour.

The archaeological record corroborates the idea and indicates that our ancestors depended on a diet heavy in shellfish and cold-water fish—both rich sources of omega-3 fatty acids. These fats may have driven the evolution of our uniquely complex brains, which are 60 percent fat in composition. One omega-3 in particular, docosahexaenoic acid, or DHA, is arguably the single nutrient most strongly associated with brain health.

In 1972 psychiatrist Michael A. Crawford, now at Imperial College London, co-published a paper concluding that the brain is dependent on DHA and that DHA sourced from the sea was critical to mammalian brain evolution, especially human brain evolution. For more than 40 years he has argued that the rising rates of brain disorders are a result of post–World War II dietary changes—especially a move toward land-sourced food and, subsequently, the embrace of low-fat diets. He feels that omega-3s from seafood were critical to the human species' rapid neural march toward higher cognition.

Many studies have confirmed DHA's importance to the development, structure and function of the human brain: it is a component of neuronal cell membranes, facilitates neuron-to-neuron communication, and is also thought to boost levels of brain-derived neurotrophic factor, a protein that supports the growth and survival of brain cells. Given the starring role this and other omega-3 fatty acids play in shaping and maintaining our most complex organ, it makes intuitive sense that incorporating more of them into our diet—by emphasizing seafood—might, as the nutritional data suggest, protect the brain from going haywire. Also of note, DHA appears to decrease chronic brain-harming inflammation.

Fatty acids aside, there is another important link between our ancestors' diets, inflammation and mental health. As we evolved, the trillions of bacteria, fungi and other microorganisms that colonize our bodies and constitute the majority of our cells came along for the ride. This so-called microbiota—and its collective genes, the microbiome—makes a critical contribution to the formation and function of our digestion and immune system. A growing number of findings now suggest that disrupting it through poor eating habits comes at a cost to the brain.

A Blow to the Gut

In one striking (if slightly nauseating) experiment in 2014, then 23-year-old student Tom Spector wiped out about a third of the bacterial species in his gut by limiting his diet to McDonald's fast food. It took only 10 days. Spector played the guinea pig for two reasons: as a project to complete his genetics degree and to provide data for his father, Tim, a genetic epidemiology professor at King's College London, who studies how processed diets affect gastrointestinal bacteria. The Spector family's research did not assess specific health consequences–they were measuring only the drop in floral diversity in Tom's gut–but Tom did report feeling lethargic and down after days of burgers, fries and sugary soda. The decline in species was so drastic that Tim sent the results to three laboratories for confirmation.

Diet-induced shifts in the microbiota of the kind Spector brought on himself can rapidly ratchet up inflammation in the gut. On top of the ill effects just described, gastrointestinal inflammation can deplete our supply of serotonin, a neurotransmitter long tied to depression and other psychiatric disorders. About 90 percent of our serotonin is produced in the gut when certain microbes interact with cells lining the gastrointestinal tract (some microbes even produce a portion of our serotonin themselves). But by-products of inflammation convert serotonin's metabolic precursor, tryptophan, to a compound that generates neurotoxic metabolites linked with depression, schizophrenia and Alzheimer's.

The good news is that dietary changes can not only wreck our microbial diversity, they can boost it, reducing gastrointestinal inflammation in the process. In 2015 a group at the University of Pittsburgh conducted a study in which 20 African-Americans from Pennsylvania swapped diets with 20 rural black South Africans. In place of their usual low-animal-fat, high-fiber diet, the Africans consumed burgers, fries, hash browns, and the like. The Americans eschewed their normal fatty foods and refined carbohydrates for beans, vegetables and fish. After just two weeks the Americans' colons were less inflamed, and fecal samples showed a 250 percent spike in butyrate-producing bacterial species. Butyrate is thought to reduce the risk of cancer. The South Africans, on the other hand, underwent microbial changes associated with increased cancer risk.

"Dietary changes are the easiest way to alter your microbiome and help to control inflammation," says psychiatrist Emily Deans of Harvard Medical School. She believes diet is every bit as important as pills and psychotherapy in managing mental illness–a view informed by her own clinical practice. "I discuss nutrition with just about all of my patients," she adds, "and I think it can really help in managing conditions like depression, at least in some people." Deans also feels that timing of meals can influence mood, and research suggests that eating on a regular schedule can improve mental health.

Deans acknowledges that science has a long way to go before we fully understand the brain-diet relation. She is also wary of the massive probiotic industry that has, like the supplement industry in general, barreled ahead of the minimal but growing scientific evidence suggesting that probiotics might be effective in preventing or treating mental illness. "You can do studies with, for example, certain vitamins, and some might turn out positive and others negative," she explains. "But the truth is vitamins exist in all sorts of different chemical states in food and in just one state in supplements." This difference in form between nutrients in food versus pills explains why the data tend to favor nutrition through diet rather than supplementation. "I think we can safely say that certain dietary patterns seem to promote a healthy microbiome," Deans speculates, "like the Mediterranean diet and diets that include lots of fiber, fermented foods and fish." And a healthy microbiome may be essential for a healthy brain.

Food for Thought

For seven years now Carolyn has been eating better–focusing on seafood and cutting back on sugar. She has lost weight, and her diabetes is under control. "It's part of a whole new way of life," she says, "knowing that what I eat can affect how I feel." That awareness is building momentum among patients and practitioners alike. In March 2015 a large team of clinicians and researchers published a report in the *Lancet Psychiatry* on behalf of the International Society for Nutritional Psychiatry Research—an organization Jacka co-founded in 2013. Citing modest therapeutic gains yielded by many psychiatric drugs, the authors called for the integration of nutrition-based approaches into mental health care. "The emerging and compelling evidence for nutrition as a crucial factor in the high prevalence and incidence of mental disorders," they wrote, "suggests that diet is as important to psychiatry as it is to cardiology, endocrinology, and gastroenterology."

Thanks to our evolutionary lineage (and plenty of fish), attention to our diets may prove critical to reversing the rising rates of mental illness around the world, lowering the proportion of people struggling with various forms of dementia, and staving off milder psychiatric symptoms and disorders. There is little doubt that eating right can help shuttle us through tough times—just as it may have done 160,000 years ago for a small group of humans huddled in coastal African caves.

One of the leading proponents of leveraging diet to better brain health, Jacka is encouraged that interventional studies—in which patients are actually "prescribed" a particular diet and tracked over time, as they were in her own SMILES study—are finally getting under way. Such research will be able to offer more definitive proof of the connection between diet and mental and cognitive well-being.

More and more doctors and patients are beginning to see dietary interventions as a beacon of hope after several decades of disappointing psychiatric drug development. Too many patients suffering from mental illness or dementia do not respond adequately to existing medications, if at all. For example, selective serotonin reuptake inhibitors such as Prozac—one of the most commonly prescribed drug classes for treating depression—appear effective only in severe cases; they are often no better than placebo for mild to moderate disease. As scientists learn more about the pathologies behind mental and cognitive disorders, new and promising therapeutic targets will surely emerge. But it is clear that nutrition-based treatment plans–free from side effects and low in cost–will also figure prominently in the future of dementia and psychiatric care.

Traditional Diets for Healthy Brains

Mediterranean

Research consistently finds the dietary patterns of cultures hugging the Mediterranean Sea to be among the healthiest in the world. Ingredients common to Greek, Italian, Spanish and Middle Eastern cuisine (below) are linked with improved cardiovascular, mental and neurological function.

- Olive oil
- Omega-3-rich fish (sardines, tuna, salmon)
- Antioxidant-rich fruits and vegetables (tomatoes, peppers, eggplant)
- Whole grains
- Legumes
- Moderate amounts of lean meat and red wine
- Limited sugar and processed food

Okinawan

According to the World Health Organization, the Japanese have the highest life expectancy in the world—in part thanks to the population of Okinawa. Staples of the island group's traditional diet (below) include the nutrient-rich purple sweet potato, often eaten in place of rice. Indeed, Okinawans tend to eat less fish, meat, rice and sugar—and fewer calories overall—than do those in other parts of the country.

- Antioxidant-rich vegetables (Okinawan purple sweet potatoes)
- Seaweed
- Some fish
- Some meat
- Limited sugar and white rice intake

Scandinavian

Swedish meatballs aside, Scandinavians cook, collect and cultivate a host of foods that together constitute the new Nordic diet, one of the world's healthiest. It is associated with reduced inflammation and decreased risk for cardiovascular disease and diabetes, both of which can influence brain health. Of particular note, Scandinavians tend to cook with canola oil, also called rapeseed oil, which contains far more omega-3 fatty acids than olive oil.

- Fruits (lingonberries)
- Vegetables (potatoes)
- Nuts/whole grains (rye breads very common)
- Seafood
- Moderate amounts of meat and dairy
- Canola (rapeseed) oil

Referenced

Mediterranean Dietary Pattern and Depression: The PREDIMED Randomized Trial. Almudena Sánchez-Villegas et al. in *BMC Medicine*, Vol. 11, Article No. 208; September 20, 2013.

Early Intervention to Preempt Major Depression among Older Black and White Adults. Charles F. Reynolds et al. in *Psychiatric Services*, Vol. 65, No. 6, pages 765–773; June 2014.

The Origins and Significance of Coastal Resource Use in Africa and Western Eurasia. Curtis W. Marean in *Journal of Human Evolution*, Vol. 77, pages 17–40; December 2014.

Nutritional Medicine as Mainstream in Psychiatry. Jerome Sarris et al. in *Lancet Psychiatry*, Vol. 2, No. 3, pages 271–274; March 2015.

Western Diet Is Associated with a Smaller Hippocampus: A Longitudinal Investigation. Felice N. Jacka et al. in *BMC Medicine*, Vol. 13, Article No. 215; September 8, 2015.

About the Author

Bret Stetka is a writer based in New York City and editorial director of Medscape Neurology (a subsidiary of WebMD). His work has appeared in Wired*, NPR and the* Atlantic*. He graduated from the University of Virginia School of Medicine in 2005.*

School-Based Online Programs Instruct Pupils about Good Mental Health

By Shekhar Saxena, Anisha Padukone

Roughly 50 percent of all mental health conditions begin before people are in their mid-teens even though most go undetected and untreated. Adding to this, suicide is one of the top causes of death in young adults. The unprecedented disruptions of the pandemic has aggravated such problems, especially for younger age groups. All of these factors mean there is no better time to support and strengthen mental health education among teenagers.

In response to these needs, the World Health Organization has recently recommended several evidence-based interventions to protect and promote the mental health of adolescents by strengthening interpersonal and emotional regulation skills. A recent review of literature also suggests ways in which children and young people could be helped by the digital delivery of mental health interventions.

One of the most effective ways of implementing mental health education is through school systems, either as a course module within a class or as a separate class within the school. A lot of research has shown the effectiveness of these programs, but we need continued studies to further develop the best curricula to put in place to supplement existing social and educational programs.

The addition of technology and digitization will ensure more personalization, active participation and the ability to provide greater outreach at affordable costs. The Live Love Laugh Foundation, a mental health nonprofit organization in India, started an adolescent mental health program called You Are Not Alone in 2016. This program aims to educate adolescents and their teachers about stress, anxiety and depression. It also suggests tips to build resilience, provide access to support and normalize conversations about mental health within school settings.

So far, the program has educated more than 200,000 students and 20,000 teachers across the country. Results from a survey revealed that 76.6 percent of students had not attended a mental health awareness session previously. And 90 percent of the students, parents and teachers who responded from 32 schools across 10 Indian states were keen to have mental health sessions conducted. In the wake of the pandemic, this program is being digitized with an educational technology partner to cater to the vast number of Indian teens using a virtual learning platform. A facilitator delivers the session using a designated module while students learn and interact using quizzes, polls, and so on.

Another example is a program run by the Mental Health Association in New York State (MHANYS). In 2016 New York passed a law that made it mandatory for schools to provide mental health instruction as part of K–12 health education. The program offers a component to educate families and caregivers about youth mental health by providing access to webinars and other online resources to promote greater understanding of mental health and to support wellness for the whole family. It is intended to serve as a model for other cities and even for whole countries to follow.

The key factors that determine the success of a digital program are an entertaining design, a high level of interactivity for its users, an ability to reach large numbers of students across diverse regions, availability in numerous languages, and economic sustainability through low-cost or free access. These steps could enable a program to reach nearly two billion children globally, most of whom are in low- and middle-income countries.

To make these projects succeed, organizers must encourage public-private partnerships, collaborations with technology and social media companies, and recruitment of celebrities and other social icons as endorsers. If these elements all coalesce, we can create a revolution in mental health education for teens.

If You Need Help

If you or someone you know is struggling or having thoughts of suicide, help is available. Call, text, or online chat 988 to be connected to a trained crisis counselor available 24/7 through the 988 Suicide & Crisis Lifeline. This new three-digit Lifeline became active in July 2022 and was formerly the National Suicide Prevention Lifeline. The old Lifeline number remains available by calling 1-800-273-TALK (8255).

This is an opinion and analysis article, and the views expressed by the author or authors are not necessarily those of Scientific American.

About the Authors

Shekhar Saxena is a professor of the practice of global mental health at the Harvard T. H. Chan School of Public Health. He is former director of mental health at the World Health Organization in Geneva.

Anisha Padukone is CEO of the Indian mental health nonprofit The Live Love Laugh Foundation.

GLOSSARY

anhedonia An inability to feel pleasure.

antidepressant A medication used to treat major depressive disorder, certain anxiety disorders, and some other mental health conditions.

atrophy To become less effective or to waste away through lack of use or neglect.

conundrum A difficult or confusing problem.

correlation A connection between two things in which one affects or is dependent upon the other.

electroencephalography (EEG) Measurement and recording of electrical activity in different parts of the brain.

epigenetics The biological study of how environment and behavior can change how genes work.

functional magnetic resonance imaging (fMRI) A technique for measuring brain activity by mapping changes in blood flow.

inordinate Excessive or beyond reasonable limits.

internalize To unconsciously learn to make a behavior or attitude a part of one's nature.

penumbra The partially-shaded outer region of a shadow.

rumination To think something over deeply, sometimes obsessively and repeatedly to the point of distraction.

stigma Something that is disapproved of or discriminated against by other members of society.

transgress To violate the moral or social boundaries of a group of people.

FURTHER INFORMATION

Adams, Char. "Study: Facing Racism Depletes Young Adults' Mental Health." NBC News, November 9, 2021, https://www.nbcnews.com/news/nbcblk/study-facing-racism-depletes-young-adults-mental-health-n1283611.

Hanson, Jolene. "Identifying Signs of Anxiety and Depression." Mayo Clinic, May 4, 2022, https://www.mayoclinichealthsystem.org/hometown-health/speaking-of-health/addressing-your-mental-health-by-identifying-the-signs-of-anxiety-and-depression.

Hogg, Teaghan, Léan O'Brien, and Samantha Stanley. "Feel Alone in Your Eco-Anxiety? Don't–It's Remarkably Common to Feel Dread About Environmental Decline." The *Conversation*, November 7, 2021, https://theconversation.com/feel-alone-in-your-eco-anxiety-dont-its-remarkably-common-to-feel-dread-about-environmental-decline-170789.

Law, Tara. "Loneliness Is a Public Health Emergency. Here's What Helps, According to Experts. *TIME*, June 1, 2022, https://time.com/6183058/loneliness-health-effects-what-to-do/.

Miller, Naseem S. "Racial Disparities in Mental Health Care: An Explainer and Research Roundup." *Journalist's Resource*, May 18, 2022, https://journalistsresource.org/home/racial-disparities-mental-health/.

Richtel, Matt, and Annie Flanagan. "'It's Life or Death': The Mental Health Crisis Among U.S. Teens." *New York Times*, April 23, 2022, https://www.nytimes.com/2022/04/23/health/mental-health-crisis-teens.html.

Saner, Emine. "Therapy v. Medication? How to Choose the Best Treatment for Anxiety." *Guardian*, May 25, 2022, https://www.theguardian.com/lifeandstyle/2022/may/25/therapy-v-medication-how-to-choose-the-best-treatment-for-anxiety.

CITATIONS

1.1 Expanding Mental Health Care Is a Medical Necessity by The Editors (December 1, 2021); 1.2 Susceptibility to Mental Illness May Have Helped Humans Adapt over the Millennia by Dana G. Smith (March 1, 2019); 1.3 Brain Imaging Identifies Different Types of Depression by Esther Landhuis (February 21, 2017); 1.4 Bad News for the Highly Intelligent by David Z. Hambrick, Madeline Marquardt (December 5, 2017); 1.5 Is Depression Just Bad Chemistry? by Hal Arkowitz, Scott O. Lilienfeld (March 1, 2014); 1.6 Is Chronic Anxiety a Learning Disorder? by Daniel Barron (October 11, 2018); 1.7 Faulty Circuits by Thomas R. Insel (April 1, 2010); 2.1 News about Racial Violence Harms Black People's Mental Health by Melba Newsome (June 8, 2021); 2.2 Pandemic Year One Saw a Dramatic Global Rise in Anxiety and Depression by Gary Stix (October 8, 2021); 2.3 Suicide Rates Rise in a Generation of Black Youth by Melinda Wenner Moyer (September 29, 2021); 2.4 Climate Anxiety and Mental Illness by Brian Barnett, Amit Anand (October 10, 2020); 2.5 The Personality Trait 'Intolerance of Uncertainty' Causes Anguish during COVID by Francine Russo (February 14, 2022); 2.6 The Scientific Underpinnings and Impacts of Shame by Annette Kämmerer (August 9, 2019); 2.7 Why the Secrets You Keep Are Hurting You by Michael Slepian (February 5, 2019); 3.1 Novel Drug Therapies Could Tackle Treatment-Resistant Depression by Husseini Manji, Joseph Hayes (September 14, 2021); 3.2 A Renaissance for Psychedelics Could Fill a Long-Standing Treatment Gap for Psychiatric Disorders by Danielle Schlosser, Thomas R. Insel (September 14, 2021); 3.3 Is an Antidepressant Right for You? Ask Your Brain Waves by Karen Weintraub (February 10, 2020); 3.4 Fighting Depression with Magnets by Kasra Zarei (December 20, 2017); 3.5 Experimental Brain Implant Could Personalize Depression Therapy by Gary Stix (October 4, 2021); 3.6 Can a Pill That Boosts "Resilience" Treat Depression? by Gary Stix (April 11, 2018); 3.7 Why I Got My Brain Zapped by David Levine (July 19, 2016); 3.8 SSRIs May Help Us See the Glass Half Full by Roni Jacobson (July 1, 2014); 4.1 Adolescent Mental Health? There's a 'Vaccine' for That by Tamar Mendelson and Laura Clary (September 7, 2021); 4.2 Can Talk Therapy Help People Who Are Unable to Experience Joy? by Dina Fine Maron (August 15, 2018); 4.3 Why Exercise May Be the Best Fix for Depression by Ferris Jabr (January 1, 2017); 4.4 Mindfulness Can Improve Your Attention and Health by Amishi P. Jha (March 1, 2013); 4.5 Evolution Could Explain Why Psychotherapy May Work for Depression by Gary Stix (February 12, 2021); 4.6 The Best Diet for Your Brain by Bret Stetka (March 1, 2016); 4.7 School-Based Online Programs Instruct Pupils about Good Mental Health by Shekhar Saxena, Anisha Padukone (September 14, 2021)

Each author biography was accurate at the time the article was originally published.

INDEX